THE EVANGELICAL DOCTOR

John Wycliffe

THE EVANGELICAL DOCTOR

John Wycliffe and the Lollards

Douglas C. Wood

 **EVANGELICAL PRESS**

EVANGELICAL PRESS,
16/18 High Street, Welwyn, Herts, AL6 9EQ, England

© Evangelical Press, 1984

First published 1984

ISBN 0 85234 188 1

Bible quotations are from the New International Version

Typeset in Great Britain by Inset, Chappel, Essex
Printed by The Pitman Press, Bath, England

To

Christine, my life-partner in the work of writing, whose criticism, help, patience and encouragement have been invaluable.

The author wishes to thank the following authors and publishers for permission to quote from their works: *Roman Catholicism* by Dr L. Boettner, published by the Presbyterian and Reformed Publishing Company, Nutley, New Jersey, U.S.A. and *The Morning Star* by G. H. W. Parker, published by Paternoster Press, Exeter, Devon.

He owes a great debt to Mr Gordon Sayer, Librarian of the Evangelical Library, London, and his staff for their generosity in supplying many valuable reference books for the work.

Contents

1. 'People that walked in darkness' — 1
2. Wycliffe and the friars — 11
3. England's leading scholar — 20
4. Clash with the pope — 25
5. 'Evangelical Doctor' — 34
6. The 'Good Parliament' — 43
7. Riot in the cathedral — 51
8. Defiance of the pope — 57
9. Accused of heresy — 66
10. Forbidden book — 75
11. Preaching the Word — 86
12. Persecution — 96
13. The gospel spreads — 106
14. Wycliffe's teaching — 112
15. Early history of the Lollards (1382—1401) — 118
16. Later history of the Lollards (1401—1521) — 127
    Bibliography — 139
    Index — 141

Illustrations

Opposite Page

John Wycliffe (Frontispiece)	iii
Painting: 'The Dawn of the Reformation' by W.F. Yeames *(Suter Gallery, New Zealand)*.	10
The Parish Church at Wycliffe, Yorkshire, where John de Wycliffe was born.	11
The Parish Church at Lutterworth.	24
The pulpit in Lutterworth church.	25
Memorial to Wycliffe in Lutterworth church.	50
Side door at Lutterworth church, through which Wycliffe's body was carried to be buried.	51
Wycliffe's Bible *(by kind permission of the Dean and Chapter of Hereford Cathedral)*.	74
The beginning of Mark's Gospel from the translation by Wycliffe *(by courtesy of the Bodleian Library)*.	75
Monument to Wycliffe at Lutterworth.	136

Cover illustrations:

Top left: Oxford, where Wycliffe studied.
Bottom left: Portrait of Wycliffe.
Centre: Monument to Wycliffe at Lutterworth.
Top right: Lutterworth Parish Church.
Bottom right: "The Dawn of the Reformation" by W.F. Yeames

1.
'People that walked in darkness'

c. 1329—1349

When fog descends on the country, it blots out all landmarks and most lights. Only the brightest lights shine through it.

From the late fifth century to about A.D. 1 000 is the period called by historians 'the Dark Ages' and nowhere was this more true than for the church. Superstition, shrines, man-made ceremonies, the worship of images and relics, and man's traditions descended upon the church like a thick fog and hid the truth of God's Word. Technically, the Dark Ages ended about A.D. 1 000, but the fog still hung over the church for several hundred years after this.

But God had 'not left himself without testimony' (Acts 14:17). Here and there a few faithful souls let their light shine through the obscurity. John Wycliffe[1] stands out as one of the brightest.

When the Holy Spirit quickened the heart and mind of Wycliffe, he rescued the Scriptures from their entombment. He then preached from them and translated the Bible into English. The awakening and the work of Wycliffe and his followers may seem small compared with the work of the other Reformers, one hundred and fifty years later, but Wycliffe laid the foundations on which others could rebuild the Christian church. He performed a vital task.

How did Christianity first reach England (or Britain as it was then called) and why did the Bible become entombed and unknown to the average man or woman of the fourteenth century? We have no clear answer to the first question. Legends and tales abound of saints who first preached the gospel to the Britons, yet history is silent. But the well-known Christian apologist and theologian Tertullian (c. 160—c. 220), and Origen (c. 185—c. 254), an important Egyptian theologian, both mention that Christianity had reached Britain by the end of the second century. About 200 Tertullian wrote, 'Parts of Britain were inaccessible to the Romans but have yielded to Christ.'

While nothing is certain, it is highly probable that the evangelization of Britain was begun by ordinary Christians, probably merchants, who came here to trade from Asia Minor, Gaul (France), Greece or Alexandria. We frequently fail to realize that many Christians in the second century still remembered our Lord's Great Commission (Matthew 28:18—20) and, like the Christians of Acts 8:4, 'preached the word wherever they went' as they carried out their normal business.

It is easy to picture an early British harbour and a group of merchants counting their profits when the trading is finished. But a few are still talking to the Britons. They have more vital things to say. They tell them about the birth, life, death and resurrection of Jesus Christ and the salvation that he offers to all who will believe. News of this kind was surely startling for the Britons but, just as surely, some were converted.

Gradually, churches were formed and when the savage Diocletian persecution began at the end of the third century, British Christians suffered for their faith. Three names have been recorded: Alban of Verulam (now St Albans), Aaron and Julius of Caerleon. Diocletian's successor, Constantine, claimed the throne of the Caesars in 306 and was the first emperor to profess to be a Christian. Persecution ceased and records of British church history then really began.

Constantine, the new Roman emperor, made a profession of Christian faith because he had marched into battle against his enemy, Maxentius, trusting in the sign of the Christian's God, and he had won the battle. He felt that here was a new and powerful God who had given him the victory and Constantine, for his part, must 'keep on the right side' of this God. Clearly then, he must favour the churches and the Christians: there must be no more persecutions. While he lived, Constantine made handsome donations to the churches and gave orders to the governors of the provinces to treat the Christians with respect.

This was a sudden swing of the pendulum. From being the most persecuted people, Christians suddenly became the most favoured. Sudden success is rarely good for anyone and it was no different for the fourth-century church. By 319 the clergy (as they were now called) were made exempt from certain public obligations. By 321 the churches could receive legacies and Sunday work was forbidden to city dwellers. In 319 private heathen sacrifices were forbidden. Large church buildings were shooting up in the big cities.

In such a climate it was inevitable that Christianity should become the 'popular' religion and pagans swarmed to the churches seeking baptism and became 'Christianized pagans'. In 324 Constantine issued an edict in which he urged his subjects to become Christians. Now it paid to be a Christian, and bishops and clergy, already living far below the apostolic spiritual standards (but far above them materially), were dazzled by their riches and honours. As a result, they grew more worldly, time-serving and materialistic. When, in 330, Constantine moved the official capital to Constantinople (now Istanbul), it left the Bishop of Rome the most conspicuous man in the old capital by the Tiber. The Latin-speaking West still looked with respect, if not reverence, to Rome and this was quite unintended by the emperor.

As early as the third century, the Roman bishops had claimed to hold an 'exceptional position'. This claim was the seed which was to grow into the papacy. About 375, Damasus I asserted the teaching authority of the Roman bishop over the other bishops, basing this on the legacy of Peter. History is silent concerning Peter and Rome. If we rely on history we may conclude that he never even visited the city. Legends and traditions abound, and on these, and on the misinterpretation of Christ's words in Matthew 16:18—20, the Roman bishops based their claim.

Not content with the success that they had achieved, the leaders in the Roman church stooped to forgery to vindicate their claim of the supremacy of Peter. A document, known as 'the Donation of Constantine', purporting to date from the fourth century but now known to be an eighth-century forgery, claimed that Constantine I ordered all clergy to be subject to Pope Sylvester and his successors. It also gave him the city of Rome and all western parts of the empire.

Soon after this, about 847, came the 'Pseudo-Isodorian Decretals', another forgery. These documents, partly decisions of early church councils and partly forged 'decisions', conferred on the Bishop of Rome supreme jurisdiction over all the churches of Christendom. They proclaimed the supremacy of the pope over the whole world, including those areas still undiscovered or unevangelized. In an uncritical, largely illiterate age, these documents passed as genuine and only the Renaissance and the Reformation showed them to be false.

What of the church in Britain? How was she faring? In those days Britain was several weeks' travel from Rome. When in 410, Alaric, the Visigoth chieftain, captured Rome, the one-time 'mistress of the world' fell to the barbarians and her empire collapsed. Her troops were withdrawn from Britain some time before this to assist in the wars with the invaders. Britain increasingly became attacked by the Nordic warriors (Jutes, Angles and Saxons) who had been invading the island since the fourth century. Much of Britain became heathen land again as the Celts were driven westwards into Wales, Cornwall and north-west England.

Unfortunately, while we see the corruption that had crept into the Roman church, we cannot pretend that the British churches were pure and apostolic. But compared to the churches of Greece, Rome or North Africa, British Christians still maintained a zeal to preach the gospel and see men and women saved. While Rome and the other churches had largely ceased to have ministers of the Word and had replaced them with priests who offered a sacrifice on an altar, Britain still had elders and bishops as leaders in the churches. Many of them still showed a zeal for evangelization and sought to convert the Picts and Scots with some measure of success.

In Britain, bishops and elders appear to have been humbler men who entertained no such ambitions as we see in the Bishop of Rome. Evangelization and teaching were their main objectives. Despite this, they were human and when the Nordic invasion swept over Britain they felt such a hatred for these barbaric invaders that they made only a few half-hearted attempts to evangelize them. So England, as it is today, was an open prey for anyone who chose to come preaching 'another gospel'.

In 597 the blow fell. A party of Roman clergy landed on the Isle of Thanet, led by Augustine, who had been sent by Pope Gregory the Great to 'evangelize' the English people. Augustine was helped by the fact that Ethelbert, King of Kent, had married a Christian princess, Bertha, of Frankish (French) descent. France was already under the heel of the pope and Bertha had brought a Frankish bishop with her as chaplain. Gregory could not have made a better choice. Augustine's main aim in life was not to save souls, but to gather all men under the Roman pontiff. Where we expect to see love, faith and holiness in a man of God, Augustine replaced these with authority, power and pride.

The missionaries soon showed how their 'gospel' differed from that preached by the apostles. When they met Ethelbert, they went in procession with a huge cross on which the figure of Christ was portrayed, while the monks followed, chanting Latin hymns. Ethelbert was most impressed and soon embraced the new faith, which now included the doctrine of purgatory. This new faith spread rapidly, so much so that Augustine reported baptizing ten thousand pagans in one day. Mass evangelization *par excellence*!

Augustine was soon consecrated Bishop of the English at Arles, on Pope Gregory's instructions. On his return to England he founded the see of Canterbury and used it as his base for evangelization. But outside Kent his progress was slow. While he claimed, on papal authority, supremacy over all Christians in Britain, this was rejected by the Welsh clergy at a conference held near the mouth of the Severn. (Welsh was the name given by the Saxons to the Celts. It is the Saxon word for 'foreigner'.)

Until the mid-seventh century the evangelists from the Church of Iona, off the Scottish coast, did much more evangelism than those from Canterbury. They worked hard to convert the English, as the Jutes, Angles and Saxons came to be called. They re-evangelized Northumbria and Essex and evangelized Mercia and the West Saxons. Some Ionian monks even reached Sussex, still a heathen county.

While the Celtic evangelists remained in Celtic territory, Rome could largely ignore their existence. But when rivalry began for Saxon Sussex, the stage was set for a confrontation between the Roman clergy and the Celtic missionaries.

When they met at the Synod of Whitby in 664, it was ostensibly to debate the main questions upon which they disagreed. These were: (1) the system of reckoning Easter; (2) the form of tonsure (head-shaving) practised by both clergy; and (3) church government (the Roman church was diocesan while the Celtic churches were monastic and tribal).

But behind all these lay the vital question: how did they regard the Bishop of Rome? While Christians in the Celtic churches looked upon him as the highest dignitary in Christendom, the Roman clergy ascribed to him judicial authority also. The Celtic clergy refused to admit this. But by argument and persuasion, King Oswy, who had summoned the synod, and numerous others, agreed to the claims of Rome. The men from Iona felt rejected and many returned to the Celtic lands, while others reluctantly agreed to the papal demands. The landslide had begun. Soon the Roman pontiff could claim all England as his, but he had to wait several centuries before the whole of the British Isles bowed to the papal sceptre.

After the raids from Vikings and other barbarians were over, the kings of Europe attempted to build up their domains and create law and order, with a reasonably fair tax system. They had two enemies: the nobles, who saw their power diminishing, and the church or, we should say, the pope. The first was easily dealt with, but the struggle with Rome lasted for hundreds of years. It was at its peak from the tenth to the sixteenth centuries.

When a man takes the title 'pontiff' (that is, 'bridge builder') or *pontifex maximus*, he elevates himself to more than a superman. This was the title used by the pagan Roman emperor, who was also the head of the old Roman religious college of pagan priests and who claimed to be the 'connecting bridge' between this life and the next. A man who does this is in fact claiming, as did Pope Leo XIII in 1885, to hold 'upon this earth the place of God Almighty'. There is but one word for this: blasphemy. Popes have been blaspheming ever since the rise of the papacy in 590. While Leo claimed this officially in 1885, it had been unofficially assumed by his predecessors for centuries. Even a Catholic priest becomes on his ordination *'alter Christus'* (another Christ') because it is claimed that he will offer on the altar the same sacrifice as did Christ.

Obviously anyone making such haughty and arrogant claims will not give way easily to the just claims of kings to hold dominion over their lands. So, when the pope gave William the Conqueror his blessing to invade England and Harold was defeated at Hastings in 1066, the pope expected obedience in return. Instead William wrote to him and said, 'I refuse to do fealty,[2] and I will not do it; for I did not promise it, nor do I find that my predecessors did fealty to yours.'[3] Instead, William merely sent the tribute money, 'Peter's pence', which made the pope exclaim, 'What value can I set on money which is contributed with so little honour?'

We need to remember that William, a Norman, was descended from the original Norsemen or Vikings who had settled in Normandy and had professed Christianity only a relatively short time. The Norsemen were proud and independent people who did not bow the knee to any man. Here, William shows his ancestry. This is but one example of the long struggle between Rome and the king.

Still the eastern part of Europe, where the emperor ruled from Constantinople, capital of the old Byzantine empire, refused to recognize the pope as head of the church. Constantinople was an old rival of Rome and for centuries the struggle for supremacy continued. The Eastern church looked instead to the Patriarch of Constantinople. Eventually, after many doctrinal quarrels and political struggles, in 1054 the Eastern church finally separated completely from Rome, ostensibly over the question of whether or not to use leavened bread in the Eucharist (communion service) and the *'filioque'* clause which had been added to the original Chalcedonian creed. But behind all this lay the struggle for supremacy by the pope as head of the church.

So the England into which John Wycliffe was born had, for nearly three centuries, known only the one 'supreme head, lawgiver and judge of the church', as the Bishop of Rome now called himself.

Wycliffe was born about 1330[4] near Richmond in Yorkshire, of parents who apparently owned property which included the village of Wycliffe-upon-Tees. It is highly probable that his parents were lords of the manor but nothing is certain as there is no record of his early life. This is easily explained when one realizes the horror with which heresy was regarded in the fourteenth century. Wycliffe's family, if they were faithful to their creed, would be quick to disown John and to destroy any documents that showed their connection with him once he was declared to be a heretic.

But what were England and the church like when John was born? There is no shortage of information concerning either of these. As one historian has said, 'The Christian world of 1350 . . . can be described as a society at the crossroads.' If this was true of Christendom, it was even more true of England.

In industry, in the cloth trade that was still growing rapidly, early capitalism was developing quickly, too. The cloth trade, according to G. M. Trevelyan, was the first trade to show capitalism, simply because the craft guilds, which had done much to improve weaving, could not cope with the rapid expansion of this trade. As a result a new type of person came into existence — the capitalist clothier. He provided the necessary capital for the trade to grow. He was also the forerunner of the Industrial Revolution, still many centuries ahead, but a man who was, socially, more modern than medieval.

The break-up of the feudal manor took place, too, at this time. Wages and farm leases were taking the place of peasants tilling their lord's fields. Gradually, an increasing number of people in the villages were, legally at least, freemen. Before this they had been semi-bondsmen to the lord of the manor. The Black Death of 1348—49, which killed so many people, speeded up this change. The English yeoman was taking the place of the medieval villein or feudal serf.

Towns and cities were expanding rapidly, although they still had their fields and cornlands. It was here, in the town, that the rich merchant resided, when he was not travelling around trading. Here, too, the master craftsman with his journeymen and apprentices lived and worked hard, subject to the craft guild. In many respects, in both town and country, the standard of living was improving.

It could have risen much faster but for that other power,

People that walked in darkness

which opposed the state and which bled off a great deal of money from prince, peasant and merchant alike. The church in the fourteenth century was utterly corrupt. It was accused of this not only by heretics, such as the Lollards, Wycliffe's followers, but by loyal churchmen. The House of Commons declared that the church owned one third of the wealth of England and thus impoverished the kingdom. Much of this money was used by the monasteries to enable the monks to live idly. Some was used to build beautiful church buildings, but most of the money was drained off into the papal purse at Rome or Avignon.

This enables us to see more clearly why, when papal power in political, as well as religious, claims reached its climax in the fourteenth century, it was challenged. This is also why even loyal churchmen felt that they should support their king and any man who raised a voice of dissent and challenged the pope's claims and demands. The man who was to lead this dissent was John Wycliffe.

As a child and youth, Wycliffe must have entered into the general religious practices and customs, riddled with superstition, in an innocent, uncritical way. Later in his writings, he openly denounced them with vivid memories of childhood. On every side he saw clergy, monks, friars, nuns and the village priest. It is estimated that they composed one-fifth of the population. Popular piety flourished and there were 'holy days' in abundance. While it is doubtful if he ever heard a sermon worthy of the name from the village priest, friars often arrived and preached vigorously. But if we are to judge from records, the ordinary clergy accused them of filling their sermons with 'idle and unedifying stories'.

However, friars and the ordinary clergy were enemies and the friars accused the bishops, clergy and monks of sloth and idleness. Theoretically, the friars should have lived by begging alms and were supposed to own no property of their own. By Wycliffe's day, however, they had wealth and treasures galore. He admired their founders' theories but soon came to condemn their practices. For some time they allied themselves with Wycliffe against the other clergy when he began his work as a reformer.

As the teachers of that day were nearly all priests or

monks, young Wycliffe probably received his first lessons at the nearest abbey. There he was schooled in readiness for Oxford. Wycliffe is known to have come under the influences of the political power of his neighbourhood. The Duke of Lancaster, John of Gaunt, was the second son of the king, Edward III. In those undemocratic days, a powerful man like John of Gaunt counted for much as patron and supporter, as Wycliffe soon discovered.

John was probably about fifteen when he entered Oxford in 1345 for the long course of study in theology that lay ahead. Various claims have been made for him by different colleges, but we cannot be certain which one he entered. His name first appears as a junior fellow at Merton College in 1356.

Prior to this, Europe and England were stricken with the Black Death, a rat-borne form of bubonic plague. It began in the Far East and spread along the trade routes to the West. It is estimated that half the population of Europe died and, when it struck England in 1348—49, one third of the people here died.

Young Wycliffe escaped unharmed, but to him it seemed like a visit from God — the Judgement Day. So great was his alarm that he spent days and nights on his knees crying to God, repenting and asking God to show him the path that he should follow. When he turned to the Bible (the Vulgate) he found the light and the path that he needed. It was then that he realized how his fellow countrymen were in complete darkness. They had no Bible and most of them could not read Latin, while many could not read at all. A new vision was given to Wycliffe. Some day he would make the Scriptures known to them, too.

---

1. There are many variations in the spelling of the name. The author has chosen that which most scholars prefer.
2. A feudal tenant's acknowledgement of fidelity to his lord.
3. H. Bettenson, *Documents of the Christian Church*, p. 217.
4. This is the date accepted by most modern scholars.

'The Dawn of the Reformation' by W.F. Yeames

The Parish Church at Wycliffe, Yorkshire, where
John de Wycliffe was born.

2.
Wycliffe and the friars

1348–1360

When young Wycliffe entered Oxford the colleges were few in number and their total membership was probably about eighty, all members being secular clergy. But surrounding the colleges were the priories and halls of the friars and monks. These had grown in the thirteenth century, had a wide influence in Oxford and, as we saw in the last chapter, were by now the sworn enemies of the 'secular clergy'.

The latter were the priests and prelates (bishops) engaged in the normal work of parishes plus an enormous army of 'clerks' who, in a largely illiterate age, were needed for a wide variety of work. The 'regular clergy' consisted mainly of monks and friars and it is important for us to note that many of the latter did not come under the authority of the local bishop. The friars and many of the monks were exempt from all authority except that of the pope.

But when Wycliffe moved to Merton College in 1356, having spent eleven years in Oxford, was there no trace of real Christianity in the university, or even memories of it? Had it never seen the light of God's Word and had England never known a preacher of the truth since she fell to William the Conqueror?

Providentially, God did not leave himself without a witness and there are two names that shine in the darkness of thirteenth and fourteenth-century England. Robert Grosseteste was raised to the see of Lincoln in 1235. He spent much of his life urging reform, preaching regularly and encouraging his clergy to do the same.

At first Grosseteste favoured the friars, who in their early days were filled with the zeal and enthusiasm of a first love. Later, his eyes were opened to their rising corruption and he condemned them. But his voice was most clearly heard denouncing the apostasy of Rome. In 1252, after addressing Parliament, he sent a letter to the nobles and people of England complaining of the encroachments of the papacy. He had already visited Pope Innocent IV to protest at the corruption of his court and the enormous fortune that was being extorted from Lincoln by visiting Franciscan friars. Grosseteste demanded reform. 'What concern is it of yours?' Innocent replied. 'Is thine eye evil, because I am good?'

Later Grosseteste declared that 'To follow a pope who rebels against the will of Christ is to separate from Christ and his body; and if ever the time should come when all men follow an erring pontiff, then will be the great apostasy ... and Rome will be the cause of an unprecedented schism.' These prophetic words, which were fulfilled at the Reformation, were seen in miniature when Wycliffe began his work of reform. Men made their choice and either followed the pope or listened to the truth brought to them by the Lollard preachers.

The very year of Grosseteste's death, 1253, he again crossed swords with the pope when Innocent ordered him to make his infant nephew a canon of Lincoln Cathedral. Grosseteste refused point-blank and said, 'After the sin of Lucifer there is none more opposed to the gospel than that which ruins souls by giving them a faithless minister. Bad pastors are the cause of unbelief, heresy and disorder.'

When Grosseteste died all England regarded him as a saint, although the pope refused to canonize him. But his words, writings and actions were still fresh in people's minds when young Wycliffe went up to Oxford.

The other name that shines in the darkness is that of Thomas Bradwardine or *'Doctor Profundus'* (the 'profound doctor') as he was known. Bradwardine could be called Wycliffe's 'spiritual father'. He was a pious and humble man but extremely gifted, not only in theology, but also in astronomy, philosophy and mathematics. The Word of God gripped Bradwardine. He became aware of its deep truths and how these truths were ignored or even contradicted by the teachings of the church. His lectures were eagerly attended at Oxford and written accounts of them circulated throughout Europe. His main theme was the sovereignty and grace of God. On every side Bradwardine heard and saw Pelagianism taught and practised.

Pelagianism was a heresy that stemmed from the teachings of a British monk named Pelagius in the fourth and fifth centuries. Basically, it taught man's natural ability to do good, the natural innocence of man, the primacy of the human will in salvation and the possibility of sinless perfection. Scripture directly contradicts this, as did the church at the Council of Ephesus in 431. Pelagianism was strongly opposed by the great teacher in the North African church, Augustine, Bishop of Hippo, who emphasized God's sovereignty, grace and our election and predestination. But the teaching was popular with some people at the time and gradually it gained ground in the teachings of the church, as the Bible was read and taught less and less. As any thoughtful person will see, it has a great appeal to the natural man, as it exalts man and pushes God into the background. By Bradwardine's and Wycliffe's day it had become largely (if not officially) the standard teaching in much of the Western church, while today it is woven into the Roman Catholic teaching in some of the canons of the Council of Trent.

With an open Bible, Bradwardine proclaimed the grace of God, not man's free will or his ability to save himself. He had found peace with God, like Martin Luther, through the letter to the Romans, so he taught that only as the Holy Spirit works in a man's heart can he be born anew and produce the fruit of the Spirit. He also emphasized the importance of election and predestination. He prayed constantly that the eyes of men would be opened to the truth. 'Alas! Nearly the whole world is walking in error in the steps of Pelagius. Arise, O Lord, and judge thy cause,' he pleaded. The Lord did arise but not until after Bradwardine's death. He was consecrated Archbishop of Canterbury only a few weeks before his death in August 1349. He was presumably killed by the Black Death.

Wycliffe matriculated at Oxford, probably soon after Bradwardine left. How much he heard directly from the 'Profound Doctor' we cannot say, but he was the man chosen by God to take up the torch and continue Bradwardine's teaching. Wycliffe later expanded and expounded the forgotten doctrines of the sovereignty of God, the grace of God and man's election.

Before Wycliffe could make any progress, he had to master Scholasticism, a form of philosophy and theology of the Middle Ages. This included Realism, Nominalism, Augustinianism and other Christian views of the natural world, the sacraments and ethics. This involved debate and reasoning in a way that we would probably regard as a waste of time. But it was the method of teaching used then and it sharpened students' minds and they learned as they debated. They then became qualified to teach others after they had graduated as a Bachelor of Arts. Wycliffe is considered to be the 'last of the schoolmen', as those skilled in Scholasticism were called. But the way that it trained him to think prepared him to look at the church, the Bible and the state with more critical eyes. This demonstrates the good that it did for John Wycliffe.

As John looked around him he soon found that there were more practical problems to deal with than the classroom debates. The mendicant friars, especially the Franciscans, were trying by cunning frauds to monopolize the people's money for the pope. Worst of all, they were luring the youths of Oxford to join their order. In 1357 Richard Fitzralph, Archbishop of Armagh, fearlessly accused the mendicants before the pope. He said that their efforts at 'sheepstealing' had caused great alarm because they had reduced the number of students at Oxford from 30,000 to 6,000. In particular, Fitzralph condemned the friars' trick of offering hospitality to freshmen, then, after gaining their confidence, making them take vows of mendicancy.[1] As the archbishop had been Chancellor of Oxford, he had a special concern for these students.

But before we go any further we may well ask, 'What were the students like at Oxford in Wycliffe's day, and what was their life like compared to that of twentieth-century students?' Well, for one thing, many of them were much younger than we would find today at a university. As we saw, Wycliffe was only fifteen when he went up to Oxford and this appears to have been common, although some students were older.

Another marked difference is the fact that the majority of students were poor, that is, extremely poor and not just short of money for little luxuries now and then. The expression 'poor scholar' was coined about that time and was a very familiar phrase in Wycliffe's day. Government grants were unknown then! As with students today in underdeveloped countries, the students were prepared to undergo much hardship for the sake of learning. They were prepared to sacrifice a lot in order that they might sit at the feet of one of the great masters and learn from him. We need to remember that printing had not been introduced and handwritten books, copied by scribes, cost a small fortune, so students had to learn by rote, memorizing long passages from the classics or the church fathers.

As one historian states, 'The medieval student, before the development of the college system had done its work, was riotous, lawless and licentious.'[2] Many learnt very little for want of books and left without taking a degree. Nearly all hoped to become clerks, if not priests. Daggers, swords and even bows and arrows were used in their conflicts between 'town and gown' — the regular fights with the people of Oxford. The High Street was the favourite place for a pitched battle. It has been rightly said that the violent habits acquired at Oxford or Cambridge helped to explain many of the violent actions of the clergy in later life.

But the college system, when it was introduced, not only gave the young men homes under the careful eye of a master; it also kept them from the evils of the tavern and brothel. Even more important in the eyes of the church, it kept them from freely discussing and propagating heresy.

However, in Wycliffe's early career it is doubtful if more than one hundred students lived in a college. The rest lived in lodging-houses and inns, where they could freely discuss anything under the sun. We can be sure that when Wycliffe began teaching biblical and reformed doctrine, the discussions went on well into the night. In retrospect, we can regard this as God's timing. If Wycliffe had begun his teaching fifty years later, it could have been suppressed much more easily by the masters.

But to return to the mendicant friars, what was their origin? While there were four distinct orders of friar, those of Dominic and Francis were the most powerful and exercised the greatest influence in England, particularly at Oxford. We will concern ourselves only with these two orders. The friars or mendicants were a comparatively late addition to the clergy, monks and nuns of Rome. They were formed into 'brotherhoods' (hence the name 'friar' — brother) in the early thirteenth century.

Their forerunners were the monks and nuns who first appeared in Egypt in the late third century and later spread to Palestine, Syria and Asia Minor before sweeping across Christendom. The movement began when certain ascetics withdrew from society and became hermits, living in caves. They soon gathered a group of followers around them. The ascetic viewed the natural world as sinful in itself, therefore he and his followers must avoid it as far as possible. Soon these hermits were regarded as 'saints'. Later, various leaders drew up codes of practice for their followers to adhere to when they entered an order. The desert was the easiest place for those living in hot climates, but less practical for those further north, so in time all established monastery buildings to isolate their followers from the 'evil' world.

We may well ask, 'Where did they get their biblical foundation for this way of life?' The short answer is, they had none. It was condemned by Paul when he saw the first signs of asceticism (1 Timothy 4:3; Colossians 2:20,23). But, of course, there was nothing original in asceticism or the founding of monasteries or convents. The idea had been present in the East and highly developed in Buddhism before the Christian church was ever founded.

As Dr L. Boettner says, 'In order to understand the Roman Catholic position regarding the grouping of men and women in monasteries and convents we must understand the basic viewpoint which underlies the system. During the Middle Ages the idea developed in Roman theology that man's work was to be divided into the natural (i.e. the secular) and the spiritual. Only the spiritual was thought to be pleasing to God. Consequently, while the natural man might be satisfied with the common virtues of daily life, the ideal was that of the mystic who in deep contemplation reached out for the spiritual. In achieving this higher life the natural was thought of not as a help but as a hindrance. The life of

Wycliffe and the friars

the monk and the nun who withdrew from society and from the workaday life of the world and retired into the quiet of the cloisters, thus losing themselves in mystic contemplation, was thought to be the higher life. There, in seclusion from the world, the image of God, which had been lost in the fall, was to be restored in its beauty. The monastic system is thus based on two false principles, namely, that celibacy is a holier state than matrimony, and that total withdrawal from the social intercourse and business life of the world is conducive to true religion.'[3]

But while monks took vows of celibacy, poverty, chastity and obedience, their vow of poverty soon became a joke, as they became extremely wealthy. As they were free from the authority of the local bishop and were answerable only to the pope, there was no risk of anyone visiting them to see if they complied with their vows, including that of chastity. Nevertheless, they considered themselves to be vastly superior to the ordinary clergy in the parish (who were known as 'secular' clergy) and were called the 'regular' clergy. They became, in most cases, extremely lazy and the 'fat monk' was a common expression.

All this prepared the way for the friars, whose founders were truly shocked by the state of the monasteries. The great wealth they had acquired and their seclusion in shutting themselves away from the world were both seen as serious wrongs. In contrast, the friars were to have no wealth and to mix with the people and teach them. These were their protests against the monks.

This ideal state lasted for but a short time. The Franciscans were founded in 1209, and entered England about 1221. They were known as Grey Friars because they wore a grey habit. The Dominicans, founded about the same time, wore a black habit and were known as Black Friars. But by Grosseteste's time, just over one hundred years later, they too had become very wealthy. However, they still considered themselves superior to the monks since they claimed to be more 'religious' or 'spiritual'.

A number of clergy, including parsons, were married. These marriages were irregular and voidable but only if challenged. English clergy had long resented the clerical celibacy that was enforced after the Norman Conquest.

The right of priests to marry was one of the remnants of the Celtic church's traditions. Other priests lived in a permanent kind of concubinage.

Thus the clergy were roughly divided into three groups: the secular clergy, the regular clergy (monks and nuns) and the friars, who were also regular clergy. As we have seen, the monks considered themselves superior to the secular clergy and the friars believed themselves to be the élite. These, then, were the people who opposed Wycliffe. Wycliffe was himself a priest and therefore spiritually on the bottom rung of the ladder in the eyes of his opponents.

When Wycliffe began preaching against the monks, for a short time the friars eagerly supported him because they were the sworn enemies of monasteries. It was only later, when his voice and pen were turned against them as well, that they realized that he would spare no one who did not seek to live according to the teachings of Scripture.

Before we leave the clergy of Wycliffe's day we should note the expression 'absentee clergy', which was often used, because many foreign archdeacons and cathedral clergy were appointed to English dioceses but, since they were foreigners, they never showed their faces in England. It is estimated that one in three of the archdeacons was a foreigner, appointed by the pope, and frequently a cardinal. Only when the pontiff sent them to England on official business did they set foot in the country. Many were French and the pope appointed several who were enemies of the king and of England. These cardinals, and other clergy, often held many offices in different countries and drew the money from each. This led to a great deal of corruption in the church and made Rome extremely wealthy.

Public resentment, voiced in Parliament, led to the passing of the first Statute of Provisors (1351), which denied the pope the right to dispose of English livings, and the first and second Statutes of Praemunire (1353, 1365), which forbad papal bulls and briefs being carried out unless the state sanctioned them. But as these were not strictly enforced they did little to stop the corruption.

When Wycliffe began his controversy with the friars we are not certain, but it would seem that his objections to them and their ways were voiced early in his career. It was,

Wycliffe and the friars

however, some twenty years before his crystallized views appeared in a treatise called *Objections to Friars*. It could be said that, from the day when he first raised voice or pen against the friars, the remainder of his life was one continual protest against them.

In an attempt to prevent the 'sheepstealing' by getting young students to enter their orders, Oxford found it necessary to refer the matter to Parliament. This resulted in an injunction from the High Court that none of the orders of friars should receive any student under eighteen and that all offenders should be punished by the king in council.

Whether it was to show Oxford's gratitude for the work that Wycliffe undertook as adversary of the friars in defence of the students, or whether it was in recognition of his prowess as a scholar, is not clear, but he was appointed Master of Balliol College from about 1359 to 1360.

1. J. Foxe, *Acts and Monuments*, Vol. II, p. 760.
2. G. M. Trevelyan, *English Social History*, p. 53.
3. L. Boettner, *Roman Catholicism*, pp. 300—301.

3.
England's leading scholar

1360–1368

Wycliffe remained as Master of Balliol until his appointment in May 1361 to the rich college living of Fillingham, in Lincolnshire, where he became rector. Now that he was Rector of Fillingham and an ordained priest, he expected to have an adequate income for continuing his studies at Oxford.

We may raise our eyebrows at his keenness to get a rich living with an adequate stipend but we should recognize that this was the accepted practice for those who needed money for further studies. The colleges that held the livings allocated them to those of their faculty whom they felt deserved such preferment. Obviously, John Wycliffe still ranked high with his college and university. As we noted earlier, there were no government grants then, and this living met Wycliffe's financial needs and enabled him to press on with his studies at Oxford for at least part of the time. Later, Wycliffe became highly critical of clergy who deserted their parishes and were guilty of 'absenteeism'. But now he simply followed the pattern set by his colleagues.

While Oxford was Wycliffe's 'first love', it is difficult to believe that he did not share his rapidly growing knowledge with the people in his parish on Sundays, or whenever he preached, for the first two years. In 1363, he obtained a licence for non-residence. This meant that he did not have to live at Fillingham any longer. About the same time he sought, and obtained, the office of prebend at Aust, just north of Bristol. But unlike all the other prebends of Aust, he was never there and presumably paid a vicar to serve in his place.

Wycliffe took full advantage of the extra time now available and pressed on with his studies in theology, which he then taught to students. As a proof of his ability, a few years later, in 1371, he came to be regarded as the most outstanding theologian and philosopher at Oxford. We should remember that at this time Oxford had surpassed Paris and all other European universities in learning. So this meant that Wycliffe was considered to be *the* scholar of Western Europe, a fact which even his opponents admitted later.

So far life appears to have been plain sailing for John. But in 1365 he ran into his first storm, which doubtless prepared him for the fiercer storms that lay ahead. In that year he was appointed Warden of Canterbury Hall (later to be incorporated in Christchurch). This hall had been founded by Simon Islip, Archbishop of Canterbury, who intended that it should have a warden and eleven scholars. The warden he had appointed was a monk named Wodehall, a man who proved most unsuitable for the post. As there were three monks from Christchurch, Canterbury, together with eight secular priests, something like civil war prevailed in the hall at times. We saw earlier the hatred that existed between the secular priests and the monks, so this is not surprising.

Islip regretted his decision, intervened in 1365 and expelled Wodehall and the three monks. He then appointed Wycliffe as warden and replaced the monks by three secular priests.[1]

Unfortunately, Archbishop Islip died in 1366 and Langham, his successor, had been a monk and the Abbot of Westminster. The expelled monks knew that they would find a sympathetic ear in Langham. The archbishop listened to their story, decided that Islip had acted improperly, expelled Wycliffe and the three secular scholars, and then reinstated Wodehall and the three monks. Wycliffe did not take this lying down. The Archbishop of Canterbury was the highest ecclesiastical power in the land, so Wycliffe appealed against his decision to the pope. But when he made his appeal, the supreme pontiff was not in Rome.

At this point we must digress for a few minutes. In the eighth century an alliance had been made between the papacy and the Frankish (French) kings Pepin and Charlemagne. There was Lombard hostility to the pope and he had enemies at Rome, too, so he needed military help. Pepin was crowned by the papal legate (the papal ambassador) in 752 but the climax came in 800 when, in St Peter's Church, Rome, Pope Leo III crowned Charlemagne as 'Emperor of the Holy Roman Empire' of the West of Christendom. The idea behind this was that there should be one state and one church, with the emperor and pontiff working closely together. The alliance worked well in the time of Charlemagne, but after that much strife existed between church and state. The crowning gave the popes the key to interfere in all political matters throughout Europe.

After the increased power that the pontiff had gained since the days of Charlemagne, the papacy had claimed and gained greater and greater power and authority until it reached its zenith in the twelfth and thirteenth centuries. But early in the fourteenth century the papacy suffered its first major set-back. In 1302, Pope Boniface VIII, drunk with the power the papacy had achieved, issued a bull, *Unam Sanctum*, which affirmed that all temporal powers are subject to the spiritual authority, as invested in the pope. The bull stated, 'We declare . . . that it is altogether necessary to salvation for every human creature to be subject to the Roman pontiff.'[2] Boniface may have believed this but the King of France certainly did not.

The arrogance of the papal claims angered many rulers but none more than Philip the Fair, King of France. He summoned the first States-General of France, in which clergy, nobles and commoners appeared. This assembly backed the king and opposed the pope, who was eventually captured and died soon afterwards, possibly from shock, as he was a very old man. Soon after this one of his successors, Clement V, moved his court to Avignon in France, in 1309, so commencing what Roman Catholic historians have called the 'Babylonian Captivity' of the church, as this lasted for nearly seventy years.

During the 'captivity', the popes were mostly nominees of the French king and were unlikely to have any sympathy with Wycliffe, an Englishman. England was at that time engaged in the first 'Hundred Years' War' with France. While, theoretically, the popes were supposed to be impartial and unprejudiced, the 'Babylonish Captivity' was nothing less than a time of servitude to the French kings.

True to form, no prompt decision was given by the pope regarding Wycliffe's appeal for reinstatement. Throughout history popes have often delayed making decisions for a long time. The case dragged on for over four years and then, in 1370, the pontiff decided in favour of Wodehall and the monks, and upheld Langham's decision. Then in 1372 the Crown confirmed this, acting under the influence of a heavy bribe of 200 marks.

While we are speaking here of a wardenship and not a bishopric, this is an example of the interference of the papacy in the appointment of bishops and other important church officers in England and elsewhere at this time.

The Statute of Provisors (1351) forbade the interference of the pope in the election of bishops and other important church officers. This act had been welcomed by the nation and the parliament that passed this intended that it should be enforced. Not so King Edward. Both Edward III and his successor Richard II decided that the best way to secure important places in the church for their friends was to work closely with the pope. He would then send his bull to confirm the appointment of the royal candidate. In return for this, the king then permitted the pope to appoint cardinals to other important offices in England, but never to bishoprics. The foreign cardinals, of course, never set foot in England but merely drew the money that was due to the minister holding that office. In the case of Wycliffe, we see money passing from the pope to the king. As historians point out, neither party felt strong enough to act independently but the pope's grip on even humble offices is seen here in his action concerning Wycliffe. We shall deal with the question of the appointment of bishops in more detail later.

What were Wycliffe's feelings about all this? Was he weary of the lengthy appeal and all the legal channels that it had to pass through? We wonder, too, if this sharpened his mind and made him more aware of the corruption in the church, especially in the papal court.

After being expelled from Canterbury Hall, John appears to have resided at Queen's College, where he continued to study and teach. But in 1368, while the case still dragged on at Avignon, he was appointed Rector of Ludgershall and relinquished Fillingham.

1. Some have argued that the John de Wycliffe appointed as warden was not the reformer. We accept the fact that there were two John de Wycliffes alive then (unrelated) but Dr R. Vaughan has shown conclusively that Wycliffe the reformer was also Warden of Canterbury Hall. For more details see R. Vaughan, *John de Wycliffe*, pp. 51–58.
2. H. Bettenson, *Documents of the Christian Church*, pp. 159–161.

The Parish Church at Lutterworth.

The pulpit in Lutterworth church.

4.
Clash with the pope

1366–1369

'Father Wycliffe! Father Wycliffe! I have an important message for you.'

Wycliffe turned at the sound of the young man's voice. His feet crackled on the rush-strewn floor as he walked over and took the scroll from the youth's hand.

He frowned as he began to read. This message was not from a friend but from a monk, hitherto unknown to Wycliffe, informing him of a demand from the pope, of the reaction to it by the king and of a parliament that had been specially summoned to discuss the matter. Wycliffe knew already of these things but the monk had outlined the decisions of Parliament and then attacked them vehemently. He not only vindicated the papal claims but challenged Wycliffe personally to refute his arguments, if he could.

As we saw earlier, Wycliffe had already made himself a marked man by criticizing the monks and friars. What more natural then that one of them who felt that he had written a masterpiece against a rebellious king and parliament should throw down the gauntlet before Wycliffe? John had already been marked by the friars as one who professed himself willing 'to defend and maintain that the sovereign may justly rule in this kingdom of England, though denying tribute to the Roman Pontiff'.[1]

Meanwhile Wycliffe's fame as a preacher had grown. While he taught students throughout the week, on Sunday he preached to the common people and, like our Lord, they heard him gladly. Wycliffe possessed that rare gift of mastering and understanding deep theological questions but was still able to present these deep truths in a simple way for the unlearned. Because of these gifts, he soon came to be known as the 'flower (or pride) of Oxford'.

The message brought to Wycliffe was not news, but the monk's attack was. He had heard about, and had pondered for some time, the pope's demand and what action the king should take. Meanwhile, rumours of all kinds circulated the country.

The previous year (1365) Pope Urban V had demanded from Edward III the payment of the tribute money that had been promised by King John in the early thirteenth century: not just payment of the 1,000 marks for that year (an enormous sum — greater than the king's own income) but also the arrears which were owed, as Edward had not paid this tribute for thirty-three years. If he failed to pay this, Edward must appear before the pontiff to answer for his disobedience to his feudal lord.

The title 'feudal lord' may surprise some people but it must be remembered that in 1213 King John, in order to protect himself from the anger of his irate subjects, had consented to hold his crown as a fief of the Roman pontiff. This meant that he promised to pay annually 1,000 marks to the pope and that he would at all times be faithful to the pontiff, 'to the blessed Peter, to the Roman church, to Pope Innocent, and to Innocent's rightful successors . . .' In return for this, John was promised protection against his angry subjects (especially the barons), by force of arms if need be. England had now become a vassal state of Rome, owing to John's treacherous action.

After John's death, the anger of the barons and, later, of Parliament, too, discouraged kings from paying this tribute money. When kings wanted papal co-operation for anything, they paid the tribute; at other times it was forgotten and there were long gaps between payments.

Edward III, when he came of age, had promptly stopped payment. A country engaged in the first Hundred Years' War with France was not going to pay tribute to a French pope! Besides, England had beaten France at the battles of Crecy and Poitiers and national pride made her loath to acknowledge any allegiance to the pontiff at Avignon, much less to pay money that could well be used against her army.

In retrospect, we see this action of Urban's as very stupid. One hundred and fifty years had passed since his predecessor had obtained John's promise, but England had not been stationary during that period. Apart from her military successes in France, she now had a properly constituted parliament, which included not only prelates and barons, but also representatives of cities, boroughs and counties.

During Edward's reign of fifty years, more than seventy parliaments had assembled. Many times the Magna Carta (Great Charter), signed by King John, had been talked about and confirmed again by people who were jealous of the liberties which they believed that document secured to them. It became increasingly necessary for a king to gain the approval of Parliament for any action that involved taxation. The back payment of 33,000 marks would have resulted in very heavy taxation indeed. So Edward, after receiving the papal demand, summoned Parliament (1366) and laid the question before it. After hearing the details of the papal demands, Parliament asked for a day to discuss the matter privately.

When they again assembled before the king, the lords, spiritual and temporal (bishops and barons) and representatives of the commons, all with one voice insisted that King John had been wrong to subject England to a foreign power without their consent. That consent had never been given and John's action was nothing less than treason and a violation of the oath which he had taken at his coronation. No, Edward must *not* pay the money and, should the pontiff proceed with his threat, all the power and resources of the nation would be placed at the king's disposal to defend his crown and England's honour.

England was developing a national pride and the first Statute of Provisors (1351) was to prevent interference from the pope in the election of bishops. Soon after this, Parliament passed the first and second Statutes of Praemunire (1353 and 1365) which forbad appeals by the clergy outside the kingdom (namely to Rome or Avignon) under the penalty of outlawry. All government, church or state, was to take place *within* England, not outside her shores.

The papacy had, in fact, reached a very important watershed. Boniface VIII's attempted interference with France and the start of the Avignon papacy marked the beginning of the decline in papal power. In 1250 Germany had refused to permit the interference of the pontiff; France too had taken an independent national stand, and now we see England 'coming of age' and refusing to submit to the pope. To be sure, the pontiff would continue to wave his sceptre over Europe with much power for many years, but never with the same absolute authority as he did in the twelfth and thirteenth centuries.

Wycliffe's face flushed with indignation as he read the monk's tirade. Was England to go back to the same state of servitude that she had known in John's reign? His mind went back to King John as he laid down the scroll. John's name was one that made every good Englishman's blood boil. He is described by one historian as 'a proved traitor and ne'er-do-well'.

The youngest son of Henry II, he was jealous of his elder brother, Richard I (the 'Lion-heart'), who became king on his father's death. Left in charge of England together with other more experienced, honourable and reliable men (while Richard went on a crusade to the Holy Land), John soon began plotting to overthrow the other statesmen. Ultimately, he hoped to make himself king while Richard was at a safe distance. This all came to nothing and John found himself in trouble. Still he continued his tricks, and conspired with King Philip of France. It looked as if he would succeed when England learned that Richard was a prisoner in an Austrian castle.

Soon, however, Richard was released and John was forced to sue for pardon. His brother let him off lightly and, unfortunately for England, nominated John as his heir. A few years later Richard died, and England found that John was its new king. Trouble followed his accession to the throne. A man with a false, selfish and cruel nature, the type of person who quickly makes enemies, he extorted money from most of his subjects by unjust methods, rich and poor, lay and clerical alike. He soon lost Normandy (until then it was held by the English Crown) and failed miserably in his attempt to regain it.

The climax came in two clashes: one with the church, the other with the state. A dispute over the election to the

Clash with the pope

see of Canterbury led John, in 1205, to a head-on clash with one of the most powerful popes, Innocent III. England and Wales were placed under an interdict in 1208. This is ecclesiastical exclusion from all sacraments, including Christian burial and other benefits. It may be imposed only by the pope and may be placed on individuals or whole nations, as in John's case. England remained under this interdict for six years and, in 1209, John himself was placed under the greater or major excommunication. This meant that he was banned from mass and, officially, became an outcast, deprived from all intercourse with other Christians.

In the Middle Ages the papal ban was no light affair for the individual or the country. This is where we see the iron hand of the corrupt church tightening ruthlessly. It was, in fact, a calamity for the nation. No church bells rang, church doors were barred, children remained unbaptized, the dead were thrust into holes without a prayer, and all statues and pictures of the saints were veiled in black.

Today we might wonder what was so terrible about this, but the superstitious people of John's day believed that their children would go to hell if they died unbaptized. In the same way, they believed that those who were buried without the priest reciting his prayers at the graveside had no hope of heaven. Even their prayers, they felt, were useless since the statues of the saints were shrouded. They were still in that darkness where people fail to realize that they may come straight to God in the name of Christ, without a priest. For them, salvation came only through the sacraments. These could not be received from lay hands, so people under an interdict became frantic to obtain the services of a priest at any price.

The pope also placed a dreadful curse upon John, which has been recorded and preserved at Rochester Cathedral. But in addition, Innocent III declared the throne vacant and encouraged Philip of France to invade England. Strangely enough, the excommunication did not appear to worry John very much. His response to the interdict was to help himself to some of the church's estates and so ease his financial worries. But the danger of a French invasion and distrust of his own barons and people at last brought John to his knees.

In Dover Cathedral, in 1213, at the feet of Cardinal Pandulph, the papal legate, John submitted to his chastisement, laid down his crown before the legate and swore to be the pope's faithful vassal and hold England merely as a fief of the papacy. John also promised to pay 1,000 marks for England and Ireland annually to swell the papal coffers.

This was the first of John's major clashes. A few years later he had strained the feudal laws almost to breaking-point and had misused the early machinery of state in order to extort money, not just money from the lords or the peasants but from all classes, rich and poor, lay and clerical alike. He then squandered it on one of his French wars.

So, in 1215, we find John at Runnymede, a small island in the Thames near Windsor, surrounded not only by the barons, but also, on the outskirts of the royal circle, by the freemen of England. There John was forced to sign a document known as the 'Magna Carta', in which he agreed to observe the 'ancient law' and to certify the privileges of the barons. While the charter went on to say other things about the City of London, the Church of England and the imprisonment of any freeman without a trial, the most important thing about it was that a king had been brought to order. A tyrant had been subjected to the very laws which he had previously altered at his will. It was, in fact, the beginning of constitutional government.

After John's death through a 'surfeit of peaches and new cider', the Great Charter played an important part in the formation of Parliament in the thirteenth century. A country which had suffered as it did under Innocent III, after being betrayed by its king, and had risen up in protest and brought that king to order, was not prepared to move backwards and become once more the slave of Rome or Avignon. She had finished with slavery in John's day.

As Wycliffe strode towards the shelf where he kept his books, his jaw set firmly. No, England would not go back! She must go forward. Progress had been made but there was still much room for improvement.

He reached up and took down a scroll. A friend had sent a summary of the speeches made in Parliament when the papal demand had been laid before it. Wycliffe spread out the scroll and read it through again, then, taking a new

Clash with the pope

scroll, he lifted his quill pen and began to write, 'I ask my reverend doctor [the monk] to refute, if he can, what I have heard has been delivered on this subject in a certain council of secular lords,' Wycliffe wrote.

In his reply, Wycliffe gave an elaborate account of the debate in the upper house of Parliament, based on the report sent to him. The first lord who spoke was evidently quick to arms and challenged the pope to force. 'Our ancestors won this realm, and held it against all foes by the sword. Let the pope come and take his tribute by force, if he can; I am ready to stand up and resist him.'

The second lord argued on more spiritual grounds: 'Christ refused all secular authority; the foxes had holes, the birds of the air had nests, but he had not where to lay his head. Let us bid the pope to follow his Master, and steadfastly oppose his claims to civil power.'

The third lord maintained that the payment of tribute is always on the ground of service rendered. 'What service has England ever received from the man who bears the title, "the servant of the servants of God"? Not spiritual edification, but the absorption of our treasure to enrich himself and his court, while he shows favour and counsel to our enemies,' he said.

Another argued that the only reason that tribute was ever paid was to reward the pope for absolving John, so his demand then was mere simony, a kind of clerical swindling, which lords both spiritual and temporal should oppose.

Yet another argued on the grounds of suzerainty.[2] 'Since the church estates amount to one-third of this realm; the pope for these estates is the king's vassal, and ought to do homage to *him*.'

As Wycliffe penned his reply to the monk, he described himself as a 'lowly and obedient son of the Roman church'. 'I protest', he wrote, 'that I desire to assert nothing that may appear unjust towards the said church, or that may reasonably offend pious ears.'

These words are very important, as they reveal the doctrinal position that Wycliffe held in 1366. So far as we know, he was then what might be termed a 'liberal Romanist', one who wanted reform in some of the practical issues, and one who certainly wished to curb the power of the arrogant pontiff. But criticism of her doctrine, separation from the great 'mother church', and antagonism to her or her teaching was not in his mind. He was, as he said, 'a lowly and obedient son of the Roman church', but when that church made outrageous demands upon his native country, his national pride and independence forced him to take up his pen against her.

It has been suggested by one nineteenth-century writer that the anonymous monk wrote the tirade and deliberately sent it to Wycliffe to make him raise his pen against the pope while his suit was pending and so ruin his chances of winning it. It will be remembered that in 1365 Wycliffe appealed to the pontiff concerning the Wardenship of Canterbury Hall; in 1366/67 he was challenged to defend the independence of England against the demands of Rome, then in 1370 the pope decided against him.

Be that as it may, the facts remain: Wycliffe was first and foremost an Englishman, and only second 'an obedient son of the church'. He was evidently quite prepared to ruin his chances of favour with the pontiff if he could but give some clear guidance to king and Parliament.

As Wycliffe summarized the arguments of the speakers in Parliament in his *Determination*, as it has been called, he concluded that the condition imposed by the pope and accepted by King John was a 'vain thing', and challenged the monk to prove that it was not. 'The day will first arrive,' Wycliffe concluded, 'in which every exaction shall cease, before the doctor will be able to establish that a stipulation such as this can ever be consistent either with honesty or with reason.'

As he finished writing the *Determination,* Wycliffe's mind went back to that other king who was humbled by the papacy. John was not the first king to be forced to bow to the papal sceptre. Two Henrys had both been humiliated by the papacy. Henry IV of Germany had been forced to stand barefooted in the snow for three days at Canossa, clad in sackcloth until the pope decided to grant him audience and absolution. His namesake, King Henry II of England, nearly a century later, also fell foul of the pope, but for a different reason.

Henry's grandfather (Henry I) and Henry IV of Germany

Clash with the pope

had both crossed swords with the pope over the question of whether the pope or the king should appoint bishops, abbots and other high churchmen to office. This was known as the *Investiture Struggle*. Eventually both kings had reached a compromise solution with the papacy. England reluctantly agreed to grant to the pope the right to invest new bishops with a spiritual staff and ring. The king, however, retained the right to receive their feudal homage as lords. It was understood, too, that the king still had the right to choose the man who was to be bishop.

This was where Henry II had made a great mistake. He had named Thomas à Becket, his Chancellor, as Archbishop of Canterbury, in 1162. In the eyes of many churchmen, this was wrong; Becket was too worldly. From his consecration, Becket set out to oppose the king and Henry felt that he had been betrayed by his former friend. For some years constant clashes continued between king and archbishop until, in 1170, after an angry outburst from Henry, four of his knights stole away and murdered Becket in his own cathedral. Henry had to do penance at his grave and Becket was canonized as a saint in record time. The cult of St Thomas the Martyr continued in England for three centuries.

Wycliffe shook his head. No, the king was not going to be humiliated as Henry had been. King and country had both grown a great deal in the last two centuries. England was rapidly becoming a consolidated nation; Saxons and Normans were fast becoming the English people. Now, England looked more to the king than to the pope, and there was greater loyalty to the throne than to the Bishop of Rome.

John Wycliffe certainly lost favour with Rome when the *Determination* was published but in this, his first triumph, he gained the affection of the king, barons and people of England. From this time on the people, especially, looked on him as the religious spokesman for England and as the advocate of their rights and privileges.

As if to prove that his interest in national matters had not in any way caused him to become dilatory in theological matters, Wycliffe went on with his studies at Oxford and took his degree as Bachelor of Divinity three years later, in 1369.

1. R. Vaughan, *John de Wycliffe*, p. 106.
2. Suzerain, meaning in this case, feudal lordship.

5.
'Evangelical Doctor'

1369–1372

Wycliffe's quiet days of study were over. No longer could he work steadily at his books or lecture his classes, unknown to England. Once the country knew that there was a priest who had lifted his pen to defend king and country, one whose first loyalty, after God, was to his native country and who was not only talented but willing to use his talents for England, all eyes turned to Oxford. When either pope or king acted, people instinctively asked, 'What will Wycliffe say about this?'

For convenience we could divide Wycliffe's active life into four phases. The first was his academic career, when he gave himself whole-heartedly to master theology and the Scholastics. Now we see him moving into the second phase, as he proceeded to defend England and attack (in some measure) the papacy, while still remaining 'a good son of the church'. For convenience, we will call this his political phase. Phases three and four will unfold as his life proceeds.

Needless to say, the *Determination* made both friends and foes for John. Many people, especially those of the nobility, were delighted to find a priest who had a reputation for scholarship and brains, and was prepared to use these for England, even at the risk of papal displeasure or, still worse, excommunication. Among these were some leading and very important statesmen.

On the other hand, most of the clergy and the bulk of the monks and friars felt that Wycliffe was a traitor to the faith. To them, first loyalty must always be to 'the holy father' at Rome or Avignon. This fanatical loyalty cut right across personal relationships, friendships and citizenship of England. Today, with many 'rebels' in the Roman church, we often fail to grasp what thoroughgoing loyalty was normally both demanded from, and given by, all servants of the pope, from deacon to cardinal. We can be sure that Wycliffe had seen what would happen before he lifted his pen and was quite prepared for the wrath of the monks and priests. Most of Oxford looked with favour, if surprise, on its leading scholar.

In some respects, Wycliffe was like a man who, coming to a quiet pool, had dropped a stone into the water, causing ripples to spread in ever-increasing circles. The stone had been dropped by his *Determination*, after which he had returned to his studies and lectures. The ripples had, however, continued to spread and, just as ripples move leaves and floating branches, so now the *Determination* began to move others in England.

While we know nothing of his life or actions for several years, in 1371 'the ripples' were still spreading. In that year Parliament presented a petition to the king and asked that all ecclesiastical persons should be excluded from offices of state, especially high offices.

Today, we would be amazed if we found that the Lord Chancellor, the Treasurer, the Keeper of the Privy Seal, the Master of the Rolls and the Chancellor of the Exchequer were all clergymen. But in Wycliffe's day this was so. Wherever the church could gain a foothold into matters of state, it pushed hard, got its foot well in and kept it there.

As one might expect, the excuse has often been made that there were few educated men willing and able to accept such offices and do the work efficiently. For many centuries in the Dark Ages, the ability to read, write and keep accounts degraded a man, reducing him, in the eyes of his fighting colleagues, to the level of a monk. In the Dark Ages, it would have been useless to look outside the church for men capable of holding the offices mentioned above. So, at that time, it was necessary for the church to assist by loaning clerks to undertake such work.

But in modern times, how have most missionaries tackled such problems? They have educated the people, slowly but surely, and have then passed on to the most capable the routine tasks when they have been considered able to carry them out. The church of Wycliffe's day, or earlier, could have done the same, as by this time the years of ignorance had almost faded away. The explanation for the clergy's behaviour, accepted by most scholars, is that the church had no desire to part with one jot or one tittle of its power in any quarter. It was even glad to retain a cleric in charge of the kitchen and larder so that the nobility and gentry might have 'spiritually' prepared food.

However, by Wycliffe's day, England was no longer content to see church and state under the heel of the mitre and cowl (priest and monk). Indignant men, from both nobility and merchants, began to voice their protests concerning the church's grasp. On hearing Parliament's demand, the king rejected it but decided to seek the opinion and advice of his council members. Most, if not all, of them, were reluctant to make any changes (the council was composed entirely of clergy) but they felt that some changes would have to be made to pacify Parliament.

William of Wykeham, the Bishop of Winchester, was Lord Chancellor and he controlled the government. In 1369, upon the renewal of war with France, England was speedily approaching the brink of economic crisis. Money was needed to pay for the war but, as they attempted to levy taxes, anger against both clergy and the papacy rose to its climax. In 1370, a wave of anti-clerical feeling swept over England, a greater wave than it had ever known before. Men felt extremely angry at the way in which the clergy were partly exempt from taxation by the state.

A new figure stepped on to the stage at this point. John of Gaunt, Duke of Lancaster, the king's third son, was one of the most powerful men in England, apart from the king himself. Not content with this, he sought to gain still more power and the anti-clerical feeling played into his hands and encouraged him to try still harder to become dominant in England. Edward III was declining rapidly and had entered his dotage, while in 1371 his son and heir, Edward, the 'Black Prince', returned from fighting in France, ill and unlikely to attempt to take up the reins of government from his father.

In February 1371, William of Wykeham fell from power and had to resign the Great Seal, which is kept by the Chancellor. The Bishop of Exeter resigned from the office of Treasurer. They were followed by all bishops and other clergy who held high office and were replaced by law officers of the Crown and laymen who had distinguished themselves by their public services. John of Gaunt, Duke of Lancaster, became their leader. He had achieved his ambition. These laymen were nominees of the lords, who were led by Lancaster and had planned to overthrow the bishops. Many of these new ministers were honest and capable, while William of Wykeham, it was later asserted, was corrupt. But the new ministers had no independent position or power to resist the corruption that the nobles soon introduced.

Unfortunately, this removal of clergy from high offices of state was but a temporary success. They soon returned and did not finally vacate these positions until the middle of the seventeenth century. It is interesting to note that Bishop Hugh Latimer, the great preacher of the Reformation, more than a century and a half later, declared in one of his sermons that 'Some of them would rather be clerks of the kitchen . . . But, with what conscience these same do so, I cannot tell.'[1]

A new but silent figure appeared at that parliament of 1371. John Wycliffe was present and he listened to the speeches and the demands made by the members but it appears that he did not speak.

At this point we may ask the question: what part did Wycliffe's writings play in bringing the English Parliament to realize how much had been taken from them by the priests? As it is difficult to place an exact date on many of his writings, it is not easy to give a dogmatic answer. But one thing is clear: the petition handed to the king was couched in language that echoes Wycliffe's words in several of his earlier writings.

Foxe, the martyrologist, has not the slightest doubt that when one of our ancient historians speaks of, and ascribes to, 'heretical counsels' the steps taken by Parliament to remove clergy from state offices, he is speaking of Wycliffe. 'It appeareth', Foxe records, 'by such as have observed the order and course of times, that this Wycliffe flourished about the year of our Lord 1371, Edward III reigning in England. For thus we do find in the Chronicles of Caxton: "In the year of our Lord, 1371," saith he, "Edward the third, King of England, in his Parliament, was against the Pope's Clergie. He willingly harkened and gave ear to the *voices and tales of heretikes*, with certain of his Counsell, conceiving and following sinister opinions against the Clergie..."[2]

A treatise called *The Regimen* [Rule] *of the Church*, which is either Wycliffe's own work or a compilation (probably by one of his disciples) taken from his writings, states, 'Neither prelates nor doctors, priests nor deacons, should hold secular offices, that is, of Chancery, Treasury, Privy Seal, and other such secular offices in the Exchequer.' The author then refers to the offices that they held in the kitchen, in accountancy and other work. Appeal is made to St Gregory, Chrysostom, Jerome and other church fathers. But above all, he appeals to our Lord's teaching on this and Paul's advice to the Corinthians.[3]

Wycliffe was clearly concerned about the *spiritual* life of priests, because in an unpublished manuscript he wrote, 'Prelates, and great worldly possessioners, are so occupied in heart about worldly lordships, and with pleas of business, that no habit of praying, of thoughtfulness on heavenly things, or the sins of their own heart, or on those of other men, may be kept among them: neither may they be found studying and preaching the gospel, nor visiting and comforting the poor.' The result of making them Chancellor or Treasurer, said Wycliffe, is that they do not only become worldly themselves, but totally unfit to rebuke the worldliness in others.[4]

These opinions were spread around with such success that they were followed by a popular tract called *Why Poor Priests have no Benefices* (benefice: church office giving an income to its holder). In using the word 'popular', we have to remember that printing had only recently been invented by the Chinese; it certainly had not reached Europe or England, so all tracts had to be handwritten. In this tract, Wycliffe refers to the practice of patrons forcing needy clergy to 'fill vain offices in their courts'. It is thought that some words in this tract ('one wise in building castles or in worldly business') refer to William of Wykeham, the former Lord Chancellor, a prelate renowned for his skill in architecture and finance. When all the facts are considered, there is little doubt that people throughout England were moved by either reading or hearing Wycliffe's teaching and this led to the changes in government in 1371.

When the changes took place, Wycliffe was probably brought into public affairs to support the royal cause. It is thought by some that the Black Prince was his patron in the early days, but after Lancaster gained power, Wycliffe was more often under John of Gaunt's protection.

The following year, 1372, was a memorable one for John. That year he became Doctor of Divinity and also Professor of Divinity. But when we say 'professor', we must be careful. According to fourteenth-century usage, it is true; but when we think of a professor today, we imagine a person who is selected to deliver lectures to students on a particular subject, who is paid a fixed salary or endowment and is provided by the college with his own lecture room or hall. Professors, in this sense, were unknown, at Oxford or elsewhere, in Wycliffe's day. Indeed, it is claimed that the first professor in any university, with an endowment, was only created about 1430. In John's time, every man who took the degree of Doctor of Divinity, became, in fourteenth-century language, a professor, and was entitled to open a hall and lecture to those who chose to attend his lectures.

Perhaps it would be as well to pause briefly and consider Oxford in the fourteenth century. Earlier we looked at students of Wycliffe's day and compared them and their lives with the average modern student of the Western world. When we look in more detail at Oxford in the fourteenth century, we will find it just as different from a modern city as the medieval student was from the modern one.

When Wycliffe became a professor, Oxford had narrow streets, with high, wood and plaster buildings that seemed almost to touch one another when one looked towards the sky. Little could be seen of the sky as one walked along the streets that were described by one writer as 'dark and filthy tunnels'. The majority of the buildings were, of course, thatched and the smoke poured forth from doors and windows, as they had no chimneys. Open sewers ran uncovered down the middle of the streets. Beggars crouched in corners begging for alms while, apart from market days, street traders were hard at work trying to sell their wares.

It is difficult for us to realize, not only what living conditions were like for the average man or woman, but also what they were like for the student. The students who gathered around a professor in those days were often so poor that, not only did he have to teach them without charging any fee, but frequently he had to assist them (if they showed promise) from his own pocket. There is an old German saying that is very apt: 'Poverty is the scholar's bride.' It is easy to see why Wycliffe needed those livings, not only to support himself, but also to enable him to help his poorest students.

When he began to lecture as Doctor of Divinity, Wycliffe undoubtedly covered many subjects in a systematic fashion. It may surprise us to find that a copious exposition of the Decalogue (Ten Commandments) was highly successful and considered in those days to be a work of vast importance and great rarity. But when we read the preface to this work, Wycliffe tells us that it was not uncommon for men 'to call God Master, forty, threescore, or fourscore years; and yet to remain ignorant of his Ten Commandments'. Apart from this, we need to remember the tangled web of rules that had been woven by the Schoolmen for the interpretation of Scripture. These either hid the truth of God's Word or made it so difficult to interpret that even priests were fearful of attempting really to understand it. Instead they preferred merely to reverence it as a sacred book. This surely reminds us of the Pharisees' behaviour in our Lord's day (Matt. 23:13; Luke 11:52).

To expound the Ten Commandments before the church in all their clarity, purity and sovereignty, was, in fact, one of the greatest services that a teacher could perform at this time. With all the corruption of the fourteenth-century church, and the ability of the priests to point to some refuge of lies, in which the guilty person could hide and convince himself that he was innocent before God, Wycliffe's words must have startled them like the blast of the trumpet for battle.

Let us read just a short extract from the *Decalogue:* 'Covet not thy neighbour's goods, despise him not, slander him not, scorn him not, belie him not, backbite him not; . . . But many think if they give a penny to a pardoner, they shall be forgiven the breaking of all the commandments of God, and therefore they take no heed how they keep them. But I say to thee for certain, though thou have priests and friars to sing for thee, and though thou each day hear many masses, and found chantries and colleges, and go on pilgrimages all thy life, and give all thy goods to pardoners: all this shall not bring thy soul to heaven.' These words must have come as a flash of light to those who walked in the darkness of medieval theology.

We can even foresee the time when the words of Tetzel, the Dominican vendor of indulgences, would rouse Martin Luther to write the ninety-five theses at Wittenburg in 1517.

> As soon as the coin in the coffer rings,
> The soul from purgatory springs

was Tetzel's trite saying.

'Giving a penny to a pardoner' was common practice, as people genuinely believed that they could buy their way to heaven, to some extent at least. By Luther's day it had become so much more common, and on a much larger scale too, while the claims made for 'pardons' or 'indulgences' were far more extravagant.

At this time Wycliffe had not given up the idea of purgatory, as is clear from his writings. But alongside this teaching there is constant reference to the one great Sacrifice. 'Have a remembrance of the goodness of God, how he made thee in his own likeness; and how Jesus Christ, both God and man, died so painful a death upon the cross, to buy man's soul out of hell, even with his own heart's blood, and to bring it to the bliss of heaven.'

Perhaps it was his constant emphasis on the work of Christ that has earned for Wycliffe the title of the 'Evangelical Doctor'. Other teachers were called *'Doctor Angelicus', 'Doctor Profundus'* and so on. But Wycliffe's constant appeal to Scripture, and above all, to the finished work of Christ, gained him the title of *'Doctor Evangelicus'*. When the title was first given to him is uncertain but it is apt.

It is writings and teachings such as those quoted above that justly earned for Wycliffe that other title, 'The Morning Star of the Reformation', because in these and his later writings he shows himself to be at one with the Reformers. In fact, as one modern historian has pointed out, 'His heirs were not Luther, Calvin or the leaders of official reform in England so much as those who championed freedom of individual belief and nonconformity in the sixteenth century and later'[5] — in other words, the Puritans.

The title 'the Morning Star of the Reformation' appears to have been given to Wycliffe by Daniel Neal, in his *History of the Puritans* (1732), but in this Neal is apparently echoing Foxe who spoke of him as 'the morning star', but in a wider and different context.

As we shall see later, Wycliffe was a man who was ahead of his time in his thinking, reasoning and teaching. Oxford, while shaking her head over some of his teachings, still looked with favour on her most brilliant scholar and professor. John, at this point, may have thought that, from now on, life would be much smoother for him, but his quiet days as lecturer were speedily drawing to a close. The *Determination*, that pebble dropped into the pool, was to lead to even more important and exciting events.

1. H. Latimer, *Sermons*, Folio, p. 171.
2. J. Foxe, *Acts and Monuments*, Vol. i, pp. 5, 6.
3. *Ecclesiae Regimen*, Cotton MSS. Titus, D.i.
4. J. Wycliffe, MS in C.C.C., Cambridge.
5. G. H. W. Parker, *The Morning Star*, p. 56. (Paternoster Press, 1965.)

6.
The 'Good Parliament'

1373—1377

Another papal evil reached its climax in Wycliffe's day. This was destined to disturb the quietness of his scholarly life. Earlier, we mentioned 'provisors' and statutes against them. To see the backcloth against which Wycliffe's fight with Rome was set, we need to examine these in more detail.

Since the Norman Conquest, there had been a continuous struggle with Rome over the question of who should appoint or 'provide' clergy to ecclesiastical posts. Should this be done by the king or by the pope? Reference was made to William the Conqueror's refusal to obey the pope and 'to do fealty' to him. If all the kings had had the same determination, English history would have been different. William would not permit any papal bull or mandate to be circulated in England until he had first inspected it. What a contrast to the wretched John, who laid his kingdom at the feet of an Italian priest!

From John's time the steady encroachments from Rome continued. 'England', remarked one of the pontiffs, 'is the pope's garden of delight.' Truly, they thought that she would provide an inexhaustible supply of fruit. But the day was fast approaching when Rome would find that England was to become barren regarding 'fruit'. The impoverishment and ignominy that she caused to England had become too great for human endurance.

One of the greatest drains on the life-blood of the country in medieval times was the practice of 'papal provisions'. This prerogative of the pope enabled him to declare at any time the next vacancy of any church benefice or office to be at his disposal. When this took place, he then appointed or 'provided' one of his favourites to the post. Needless to say, such benefices were always ones which drew a large revenue from the church's annual income and from this money the pope received a high percentage. In some cases he took the whole of the first year's stipend or salary. The people appointed to these offices were nearly always foreigners; some were only boys and none spoke English or set foot in the country unless they were cardinals sent to England on papal business. It was just a smart way of swelling the papacy's coffers.

Apart from appointing foreigners, another cunning ruse used to obtain money was to make a newly created bishop pay all his first year's emolument or income to Rome. In addition, the pope moved a large number (if not all) of the other bishops to new sees. In this way he gained all their first year's salaries, instead of one salary only. Small wonder that the papacy grew so wealthy!

Times had changed in many ways. We saw the humiliation that King Henry had suffered after Becket's death. 'Like people, like king,' and his subjects submitted without protest to the infliction of penance for spiritual offences by the bishops' courts. But it would have been a bold prelate who proposed to humiliate John of Gaunt in this way for some offence. People in general followed the stand taken by their leaders. The result was that a compromise had been reached. Instead of 'doing penance', as their fathers had, in many cases people paid a fine for their penance, and so made the church even richer. The hierarchy were now using sin, the enemy of the Christian and the church, to obtain more money, rather than fighting it and preaching against it. The friars, especially, used the confessional (where sin was confessed before a priest or friar) to get money from people to make their order rich.

While the poor could not do this, the wealthy sometimes paid lump sums to the corrupt church courts. This was to prevent any enquiry into their lives, a kind of blanket insurance cover that permitted them to live immorally, in every sense of the word.

While Parliament was not so concerned about the moral state of England, it protested loudly about the drain of money from the country. In 1351 the first Statute of Provisors was passed, which denied the pope the right to dispose of English livings and appoint whoever he wished. Only if the king and the chapters or patrons approved could such appointments take effect. The first and second Statutes of Praemunire were passed in 1351 and 1365. These laws began to close the doors of appeal to the Roman courts. Finally, in 1393, the third Statute of Praemunire laid down heavy penalties for any who bought or distributed papal bulls or pronounced sentences of excommunication, or for any act that infringed upon the rights of the Crown. This third Statute of Praemunire, as one old historian says, 'gave the pope a fit of fever'.

But the earlier acts passed in Edward's reign were of little effect, since he wanted to maintain his working agreement with the pope. Throughout the fourteenth century the men appointed to the English episcopate were nearly all of English stock. The king chose them and then secured the pope's approval. This does not mean that the right people were chosen. When, in 1345, Edward nominated as Bishop of Durham one of his secretaries, a man totally unsuitable for the office, the pope confirmed his appointment. 'If the King of England had nominated an ass, I would have accepted him,' the pontiff declared to his astonished courtiers.

Words would not satisfy Parliament; action was demanded. So commissioners were appointed to visit the pope in 1373. Gilbert, Bishop of Bangor, Bolton, a monk of Dunholm, and two laymen were selected. They were instructed to demand that 'the pontiff shall abstain from all reservations of benefices in our English church; . . . and that in the case of electing a bishop, it shall be enough that his election be confirmed by his metropolitan [archbishop], as was the ancient custom'. 'Ancient custom' refers to the days before the papacy presumed to encroach on England or other nations.

The commissioners met Pope Gregory XI at Avignon and he conceded that the proceedings in recent years had not been conducted in all cases in the most orderly manner possible. He admitted that some ground for complaint existed. Many excellent promises were made in much flowery language and with this the commission had to be content. Not so Parliament. It was very displeased and even held an enquiry as to the exact number of benefices that had passed into the hands of foreigners in the past year by means of provisors.

No statistics survive from this enquiry but without delay another embassy was appointed in 1374 to present a second and stronger protest to the pontiff. Again Gilbert, Bishop of Bangor, was chosen but Parliament had been searching for a man who could give this new commission the extra degree of strength needed for success. They decided that Wycliffe was just the man. His learning, patriotism and courage in disputes, plus his published argument against the King John tribute, were well known in England. Wycliffe agreed to become the other commissioner.

The papal court then sat at Avignon. To go there was second best to seeing Rome but it would at least have let Wycliffe see the heart of the system with all its corruption and hypocrisy. However, even this was denied him. Instead, Bruges, the chief city of Flanders, was chosen for the conference.

The reason why Bruges was selected appears to have been that a political conference was already in progress in the city. John of Gaunt and other English ambassadors were debating with the French the terms for peace. Papal, English and French dignitaries crowded the city, so it saved some of them from travelling any further. In addition, it was a convenient distance from Avignon and the papal court. As has been remarked by one historian, 'The spiritual governors of the world seem, in those days, to have been most wisely reluctant to expose the manners and habits of themselves or their dependents to the close inspection of enlightened or virtuous strangers.' No doubt Wycliffe's reputation had gone before him.

While we have no documentary evidence, everything points to the likelihood that it was at Bruges that Wycliffe first became friendly with John of Gaunt, if in fact they did not already know one another. It is easy to picture Wycliffe and the duke meeting in some house or inn to discuss the questions which were then on every Englishman's lips. This would explain the eagerness that Gaunt showed to save Wycliffe soon after this, when his life became endangered.

The 'Good Parliament'

Gilbert and Wycliffe met His Holiness and long discussions ensued. No records survive of these. Nothing worth talking about came from them. Gregory agreed to give way a little on the question of benefices but firmly maintained that he was both proprietor and owner of England, the king being only his tenant and vassal. That claim has remained unchanged for centuries. The only matter of real importance that can be sifted from this evidence is that the pontiff admitted some errors on the part of his ambassadors. But no admission of error was made concerning the principles which lay behind those actions. A series of letters resulted between Avignon and England in which the pope yielded a few minor points. This was the only practical result of the conference. Basically, the papal claims remained unchanged.

This double-talk disgusted Wycliffe and he returned from Bruges much as Luther did from his visit to Rome. Instead of peace and love, he had found strife, worldliness and lies. But the revelation of what the Roman pontiff was really like and the corruption that surrounded him must have broadened Wycliffe's horizons and given him a better idea of what he had to fight. Furthermore, the tenacity which the pope displayed in holding on to his claims to England and her people made Wycliffe realize that here was a foe who must be fought to the bitter end if England were to remain free.

He had clear evidence of the continuing corruption, for soon after his return from Bruges, his companion, Gilbert, Bishop of Bangor, was translated to the see of Hereford. This 'promotion' was, of course, by means of papal provisors, one of the very things against which he had been sent to protest. It would appear that Gilbert was hand in glove with the pontiff.

Wycliffe was not destined to climb so high by ecclesiastical standards. He was promised, but not given, a prebend at Lincoln. In 1375 he was passed over for the bishopric of Worcester. However, he became Rector of Lutterworth in exchange for Ludgershall in 1374. He held this living until his death.

This was surely God's providence. If Wycliffe had become a bishop he would not have had the time to give to the great work that lay before him. As it was, he entered into his teaching ministry at Oxford and his preaching at Lutterworth with even greater zeal. His views on the errors and heresies of the church daily became clearer. He has been compared by some writers to that reformer of the fourth century, Athanasius.

If the Bishop of Bangor was pleased with the results of the visit to the pope, Parliament was not. It was angry at the compromise that had been obtained at Bruges. The parliament that sat in 1376 has been called 'the Good Parliament'. It obtained this name largely through its strong protests against the papacy. The members denounced the papal demands in the boldest possible language. 'The clerks sent from Rome are more dangerous for the kingdom than Jews or Saracens,' they declared. 'God hath given his sheep to the pope, to be pastured, and not to be shorn or shaven; and that lay-patrons perceiving the simony and covetousness of the pope, do thereby learn to sell their benefices to mere brutes, no otherwise than Christ was sold to the Jews.'[1]

They declared that the only way to protect England from complete ruin and perpetual poverty was to oppose rigorously the provisors of the pope and ensure that 'no papal collector or proctor should remain in England, upon pain of life and limb, and that no Englishman, on the like pain, should become such collector or proctor, or remain at the court of Rome'.[2]

Much obscurity surrounds this parliament, but these records have survived to show that our ancestors had a clear enough discernment of the ways of Rome. They certainly did not lack courage to denounce and resist the corrupt power that had stretched out its greedy hands throughout Christendom. At this time Rome received about five times as much in taxes as did the king. England was just concluding one of the phases of the first Hundred Years' War with France and the papacy was using some of the money gained to ransom prisoners from England. It would be a strange parliament that did not become angry when it saw the nation's money going to help her enemy.

We may wonder at the obscurity of much of the Good Parliament's proceedings and decisions. The reason behind this is simple. John of Gaunt had risen to such a position of power that he did not wish to see the Commons take the initiative. Edward had become senile, degenerate and dotingly submissive to his favourite son, John. Furthermore, he had a mistress, Alice Perrers, who was in league with Gaunt. The Black Prince, the heir apparent, died that year (1376), so leaving the way open for Gaunt to exercise his power over the old king. Alice Perrers and various other favourites had been banished from court earlier that year and the bishops had orders to excommunicate her if she returned. But fortunes had changed in a few months. John of Gaunt's power had risen again after the Black Prince's death and Alice Perrers returned to court, together with other of Edward's favourites. The bishops did nothing. Under the influence of his favourites, the king declared that the Good Parliament was no parliament, in the legal sense. All its acts were cancelled and no record exists in the statute book of the greatest assembly of that period.

One thing stands out clearly. John of Gaunt's objective was to accentuate the long-standing quarrel between the church and the Commons. He hoped that this would serve as a smoke-screen for his own faults and those of his friends. We noted earlier the resignation of Wykeham, Bishop of Winchester, as Chancellor. Now, in October and November 1376, a great council sat to try the bishop on charges of corruption during his chancellorship. By standing on his episcopal privileges, he avoided imprisonment but was banished from Court and his goods confiscated. Wykeham wandered homeless through his bishopric and, partly because of popular sympathy for his sufferings and hatred for John of Gaunt, the bishops rose to a height of popularity in London which they were never to reach again. We will look at this in more detail in the next chapter.

At this time, the gifted pen of Wycliffe was used rather unwisely. He endorsed the council's actions and condemned the bishop as a 'Caesarean cleric', a mere servant of Caesar who was all out for worldly gain. Wycliffe had returned from Bruges convinced that the pontiff was a dishonest man and began to denounce Rome more loudly than before.

The disgraced Wykeham had a close friend in the young, and apparently popular, Bishop of London, Courtenay, a younger son of the Earl of Devon. He showed all the violent temper and overbearing manners of a nobleman of that period. Add to this his furious opposition to John of Gaunt and hatred of heretics, and the scene was set for a clash with Wycliffe.

Some years before, Wycliffe had written a book called *De Dominio Civili*, a scholastic argument to secularize church property. This was not overlooked by John of Gaunt. He and Lord Percy invited Wycliffe to preach in London on the subject of disendowment. Wycliffe made good use of this opportunity and went from church to church in London, presenting the matter clearly and boldly to the people.

For a proud and fierce man like Courtenay this was the crowning insult. When he learned that he and his clergy had been attacked by an unauthorized priest from Oxford, he wanted to take immediate action. Sudbury, Archbishop of Canterbury, who desired a quiet life, tried to restrain him but Courtenay refused to listen. Reluctantly, Sudbury summoned Wycliffe to appear before him and Courtenay at St Paul's Cathedral in February 1377 to answer the charge of heresy.

1. J. Foxe, *Acts and Monuments*, Vol. 1, p. 561.
2. *Ibid*, p. 561.

Memorial to Wycliffe in Lutterworth church.

Side door at Lutterworth church, through which Wycliffe's body was carried to be buried.

7.
Riot in the cathedral

1377—1379 (1)

'Lord Percy, if I had known what masteries you would have kept in the church, I would have stopped you from coming hither!' Courtenay rasped in anger.

Lancaster, who had accompanied Wycliffe and Lord Percy, coldly replied, 'He shall keep such masteries here though you say "Nay".'

Wycliffe had answered the summons from the archbishop to St Paul's Cathedral and, accompanied by Lord Percy, the King's Marshal, the Duke of Lancaster and a number of the duke's armed retainers, he arrived at the door of the old cathedral (later to be destroyed by the Great Fire of London). A crowd blocked the doorway and a sea of hostile faces greeted the party that forced its way down the thronged aisle. Wycliffe and his friends experienced great difficulty in moving anywhere inside the cathedral, because of the mob composed of the apprentices and merchants of London.

The summons Wycliffe had received was in fact an act of defiance by the bishops to John of Gaunt's power in England, and the pope had no hand in this first attack on the reformer.

Wycliffe and his companions struggled towards the Lady Chapel, where the conclave of prelates were sitting, while four friars, who represented the different orders, walked behind them. They came to act as Wycliffe's counsel, similar to the 'prisoner's friend' in a court martial. But logic and learning were not the primary weapons to be used here. John of Gaunt and Lord Percy were the most powerful men in England and, although this was an ecclesiastical matter, they intended to make their power felt. Wycliffe, however, did not put his trust in them but in God and in the Scriptures that he had studied so carefully.

With all the pride for which the Percys were renowned, the marshal thrust the merchants and the apprentices aside to make way for Wycliffe and the duke. As they approached the Lady Chapel the enormous throng that surrounded the doors glared, hissed and booed at John of Gaunt as the enemy of their liberties, it being a common practice for Londoners to show violence to their enemies. For the time being the mob forgot the favour that they had recently shown to Wycliffe and his doctrines.

'Let not the sight of these bishops make you shrink a hair's breadth in your profession of faith, for they are unlearned,' Lancaster said to the reformer. 'As for this concourse of people, fear nothing, we are here to defend you.'

Courtenay then emerged from the Lady Chapel and the first clash erupted between the bishop and the two nobles. When they eventually entered the chapel itself, Lord Percy and the duke sat down and Percy told Wycliffe to be seated also. Courtenay exploded with rage and shouted, 'It is unreasonable that one cited to appear before a bishop should sit down during his answer. He must and shall stand.'

Lancaster supported Percy and declared, 'His motion for Wycliffe is but reasonable; and as for you, my lord bishop, who are grown so proud and arrogant, I will bring down the pride, not of you alone, but of all the prelacy in England.'

'Do your worst, sir,' Courtenay challenged.

The duke angrily retorted, 'Thou bearest thyself so brag upon thy parents, which shall not be able to keep thee: they shall have enough to do to help themselves.'

'My confidence,' the bishop replied, 'is not in my parents nor in any man else, but only in God, in whom I trust, by whose assistance I will be bold to speak the truth.'

To Lancaster, these words reeked of hypocrisy and, seeing that he was getting nowhere, he turned to one of his attendants and said, 'Rather than I will take these words at his hands, I will pluck the bishop by the hair out of the church.'[1]

The waiting crowd overheard this threat and an uproar ensued, since Courtenay was a favourite with the people.

A general mêlée broke out between the duke's retainers and the citizens of London. Hope of restoring law and order was abandoned. Lord Percy and the duke escaped with difficulty, taking Wycliffe with them, and the assembly broke up in great confusion.

Throughout this verbal battle between the nobles and Courtenay, Wycliffe remained calm and silent. Archbishop Sudbury also appears to have remained silent during the altercation between Courtenay and the nobles.

Wycliffe is described by Lechler as 'a tall thin figure covered with a light gown of black colour, with a girdle about his body; the head adorned with a full flowing beard, exhibiting features keen and sharply cut; the eye clear and penetrating; the lips firmly closed in token of resolution — the whole man wearing an aspect of lofty earnestness, and replete with dignity and character'.

By contrast, the duke and Courtenay displayed little dignity when they confronted one another in the cathedral. It was also sadly lacking in the crowd's behaviour at St Paul's. This, at first glance, is somewhat puzzling when the historian monk, Walsingham, recounts that even at this time the Londoners were nearly all Lollards, the name later given to Wycliffe's followers. While this is possibly somewhat of an exaggeration, it is nevertheless true that only a short time before this incident Wycliffe had been invited to London to preach on the matter of disendowment. At that time he had been welcomed by the Londoners. Why then the sudden change of attitude? The answer can be found by looking more closely at the plans and ambitions of Courtenay and John of Gaunt.

The Good Parliament of 1376, mentioned earlier, planned, among other things, to curb John of Gaunt's power. This parliament prepared and passed a scheme to ensure that the duke kept only his rightful place in the government of England. Councillors were chosen to advise the king, the most important being the Earl of March, Lord Percy, Archbishop Sudbury, Bishop Courtenay and Bishop Wykeham.

Lord Percy became a turncoat and went over to Lancaster's side. What happened to Wykeham has already been outlined and, soon after this, the council was dissolved. Bishop Courtenay was not, however, a man who would forgive and forget. From that time he became the sworn enemy of the Duke of Lancaster and his followers. Courtenay was an extremely proud and domineering man, the more so because of his prestigious family (to which Lancaster referred during the confrontation at St Paul's). His father was the powerful Hugh Courtenay, Earl of Devonshire, and his family claimed to be descended from Charlemagne, the first emperor of the Holy Roman Empire.

With Gaunt's threat of disendowment coupled to the insults that he felt he had received from the duke, Courtenay was prepared for 'total war' with Lancaster. He had, as did others, good reason to suspect Gaunt of plans to disinherit the son of the Black Prince and seize the crown for himself.

But money also played a big part in all this. For centuries the church had received huge annual sums of money from endowments left her by the rich. This was a common practice. Not only churches, but also abbeys and priories – in fact, anything connected with the church – were frequently endowed by the faithful with large sums of money.

In the 1370s, as the war with France continued, England became in greater need of money and the church's wealth was so glaringly obvious that several times Parliament had considered the matter of disendowment. They would relieve the church of her burden of too much money.

It may well be argued that, in some measure at least, the gentry and nobility had a natural right to the money if any form of confiscation were effected. The lords in fact declared that, if the church abused the charity of their ancestors, they had a right to take back their gifts.

This met with Wycliffe's entire favour. Restitution to the people who had made the church wealthy should relieve the pressure of taxation on the poor. In any case, he believed that Christ did not intend the church to be wealthy. Views such as this, while making him popular with Parliament, John of Gaunt and the people, certainly lowered his popularity (if he had any) among the clergy.

But Gaunt had been behind a bill, then before Parliament, which was obnoxious to all citizens of London. It would, if passed, take the government of London from the mayor and put it into the hands of the King's Marshal, Lord Percy. The lives and liberties of Londoners were at stake, since

Percy was but a puppet of John of Gaunt. Since the prelates were threatened by disendowment, the people of London felt that they had a natural ally in Courtenay, and when Wycliffe appeared in the company of politicians like Gaunt and Percy, his popularity rapidly dropped.

The day after the riot in St Paul's, leading citizens in London met to consider their position. What course of action should they take? The disgraceful scene would have been reported to the king and, even as they talked, the hateful bill that would destroy their liberty was being debated.

Suddenly, two of the duke's supporters appeared, namely Lord Bryan and Lord Fitzwalter. Feelings ran high and the mob had to be restrained from attacking them. The two peers, however, had come on a friendly mission because they were citizens of London and did not want Gaunt to take away their rights. They warned the people that Lord Percy had already assumed the office of magistrate without waiting for the bill to become law. He had just imprisoned a man in the house of the marshal.

This put the match to the gunpowder. The mob snatched up their arms and rushed to the marshal's house, broke down the doors, and released the prisoner. They searched high and low for Lord Percy, even under the beds. Fortunately for Percy, he was dining with Gaunt at another house in the city. Wild with fear, a messenger burst in upon them and warned them to flee for their lives. The duke and Percy rushed down to the River Thames, grabbed a boat and crossed over to Kennington Palace on the south bank. This had been the Black Prince's home and his widow still lived there. Despite old grievances, she gave them shelter.

Meanwhile the mob, who refused to listen to any calls for restraint on the part of the leading citizens, swept out of the city gates to the Savoy. This magnificent palace stood half-way between the City of London and Westminster. It had belonged to many generations of earls and dukes of Lancaster and had beautiful lawns that ran down to the River Thames with pleasure gardens in which Chaucer delighted.

The rioters rushed to the Savoy, hoping to find and kill John of Gaunt. On the way they met a priest who stupidly reviled Peter de la Mare as a traitor. (Peter de la

Mare was the hero of the Commons and the people. He was then in prison at the instigation of Lancaster.) In a fit of fury the rioters beat the wretched priest to death.

News of this tumult reached Courtenay's ears and he hurried to the scene and persuaded the crowd to disperse. They contented themselves with reversing the arms of the duke over a shop in Cheapside, as those of a traitor, and insulting any of the duke's retainers that they met.

Riots were commonplace and, after the dust had settled, the king politely received a deputation of Londoners who expressed their grievances to him, after which the obnoxious bill quietly disappeared. He promised that their liberties should henceforth be respected and for a while John of Gaunt had to walk very carefully.

But what of Wycliffe? It appears to be an open question what happened to him after the mêlée at the cathedral. Some think that he was later interrogated by the prelates and dismissed with a curt warning not to preach his 'new' doctrines again. Others believe that he quietly returned to Oxford and resumed his teaching.

But public opinion favoured Wycliffe. 'If he is guilty,' people asked, 'why is he not punished? If he is innocent, why is he ordered to be silent? If he is the weakest in power, he is the strongest in truth.'

Meanwhile, Wycliffe continued his work at Oxford. It is unknown if he had even wished the duke to accompany him to the proposed trial. He made no reference to this incident in any of his works, though he had much to say about the later persecutions that he suffered.

It was not long, however, before the duke once more regained the supremacy that he coveted as the old king's favourite. But this supremacy would only last while the king lived. On 19 June 1377, the see of Winchester was restored to William of Wykeham, a sure sign of imminent political changes. Then, on 21 June, Edward III died and his grandson, Richard of Bourdeaux — a mere boy of ten — acceded to the throne.

What did the future hold for Wycliffe?

---

1. J. Foxe, *Acts and Monuments*, Vol. i, p. 558.

8.
Defiance of the pope

1377–1379 (2)

Ten was hardly the ideal age to ascend to the throne in the fourteenth century. Richard II's grandfather had left him one good heritage: England had not known civil war for many years. Walsingham, the chronicler, hailed the young king's accession as 'the long-awaited day of renewal of peace and of the laws of the land, long exiled by the weakness of an aged king and the greed of his courtiers and servants'. The chronicler saw the future through rose-tinted spectacles. A king of ten would be weak and he lived in troubled times. The intermittent war with France had caused the lords to maintain large private armies (England then had no standing army). Obviously these could be used against others besides France.

But what of John of Gaunt? He had long been suspected of plotting to take the crown for himself. Would he now take his chance and seize the throne? This question haunted the nobility and gave them many sleepless nights. But, no, Gaunt, as Steward of England, organized the coronation of the boy king in 1377. This was an impressive affair, designed to usher in a new period of harmony.

The Duke of Lancaster appeared to be Richard's most loyal supporter but for roughly twenty years he would continue to cast a dark shadow over the land. If he left London, people began to suspect that trouble was brewing. Such was the reputation that he had gained by his past behaviour. Even while his grandfather still lay in state, Richard had acted the part of peacemaker between John of Gaunt and William of Wykeham. He had done the same between Gaunt and the citizens of London. Lancaster had actually stepped forward in Richard's presence and embraced the members of a deputation from the City of London. Peter de la Mare had been released from Nottingham Castle and everything now looked promising.

In the banquet held in Westminster Hall, which followed the coronation, the duke and Lord Percy had to ride up and down the hall on horses to clear a way for the servants who carried the dishes. A fountain running with wine played in the palace grounds and people of all classes were invited to come and drink as much as they wanted.

But the first rumblings of trouble were heard even at Richard's coronation. The French celebrated this event by raiding England and people grumbled at the inefficiency of their leaders. They had paid enough in taxes. Why could not the French be kept at bay?

A new policy came into being four days after the coronation. A council was chosen from which John of Gaunt and Lord Percy (who had now been raised to the earldom of Northumberland by the young king) were pointedly excluded. The council was appointed to govern England until the boy king came of age. Gaunt decided to retire to private life for the present but told the king that, if he was needed, he had the greatest army in England. He appears to have thought that it would be better if Richard found out by hard experience how difficult it was to rule the realm. Earl Percy also decided that his affairs in the north urgently needed his attention, and resigned his marshal's staff.

The rumblings of trouble heard at the coronation grew louder as the year proceeded. Combined French and Spanish fleets cruised the English Channel and sacked Plymouth, Dartmouth and Rye. Despite the courage and skill shown by the English bowmen, when they beat the French army at Crecy and Poitiers, it would be some centuries before anyone could make the claim that 'Britannia ruled the waves'. She certainly did not do so in Wycliffe's day.

A French army landed in Sussex and retired only to avoid the winter storms, while they captured the Isle of Wight. Was this what a boy king was to bring to England? Some wondered if John of Gaunt should be recalled to defend his country. The following year, when spring arrived,

Defiance of the pope

gloom returned with it. Parliament ordered the Mayor of Oxford to mend the walls and towers of the city 'lest our enemies, the French, invade the kingdom of England'.

Two weeks after this order, the government was forced to haul down its flag of defiance to Lancaster. A council, supported by Parliament and presided over by his bitterest enemies, made a truce with Gaunt. They admitted that they were unable to continue the French war without his aid. On his own terms Gaunt agreed to lead an expedition to St Malo. While Lancaster had not recovered his old position, he had once more obtained some share of power.

Before returning to Oxford and Wycliffe, we must take a brief glance overseas. In the winter of 1376—77, Pope Gregory XI set sail from Marseilles for Rome. After he had landed, Gregory walked through the ruins of the 'eternal city'. The Lateran Palace, where his predecessors had ruled the church, was little more than a pile of rubble. He eventually chose a site near St Peter's for his residence and set up court. So ended the 'Babylonian Captivity' of seventy years at Avignon.

After a few months at Rome, Gregory became concerned at the teachings of John Wycliffe and issued five bulls in condemnation (June 1377). He sent three to Archbishop Sudbury and the Bishop of London, one to the king and one to the University of Oxford. All these contained vehement accusations of 'erroneous and heretical doctrines' in England, chiefly through the work of Wycliffe.

It is thought that the news of Courtenay's and Sudbury's failure at the riotous scene at St Paul's induced Gregory to issue these bulls. Perhaps he felt that if his clergy failed him at times like this he must show that he would not permit a rebellious priest to continue writing and preaching in this way. The main thing in his eyes was that the heretic, Wycliffe, stood for England against Rome and for the state against the church.

In the bulls he re-emphasized that he, Gregory, had the power to bind and loose. Wycliffe had suggested that the state should secularize the church property when she grew rich. He had also maintained that any ordained priest had the power to administer any sacrament. Rome reserved some of her seven sacraments for the bishops alone. Wycliffe's teaching smacked too much of presbyterianism — government by elders — as used by the early church, and this was anathema to the hierarchical system that the pope headed.

Bishop Courtenay received the bulls with delight. He had long known that Wycliffe's teaching undermined the power of the medieval church and it must stand or fall with the power of the pope. Now that the pontiff had returned to Rome, away from the French, he would surely take more drastic steps to suppress this heretic. If this question is considered from Wycliffe's viewpoint it can be seen that he could not expect England to defend him by force of arms as she lacked the power. The pope could easily raise a crusading army against a country that defended one declared to be a heretic.

It has already been noted that various Englishmen protested in Parliament against the papal abuses and sometimes it would appear that they were not far from complete rebellion against the Vatican. Why then did they not anticipate Henry VIII and break with Rome? But, as has been pointed out, the pope could easily have proclaimed a crusade against this nation of heretics. With England already at war with three leading nations in Europe, a crusade would have stimulated the zeal of these and other countries, and England would almost certainly have been beaten.

Apart from this, the great fundamental of medieval thought loomed large in everyone's mind — the catholicity of the church: the pope, who called himself 'the Vicar of Christ', was to them the visible and outward sign of this. To break away from the Holy Father would have been an unforgivable sin to the majority. Back in England, Rome had Bishop Courtenay as defender of the church and champion of the claims of the papacy.

To show that many in the English Parliament believed in the theory that the king was above the pope, one incident should be considered. In 1366 Pope Gregory XI issued a bull of interdict against all Florentines. King Edward did much business with merchants from Florence and decided to take those in England under his wings. In defiance of the king, Courtenay published the papal bull at St Paul's Cross and excommunicated all Florentines in England. For this the King's Chancellor summoned him and asked why he

Defiance of the pope

had dared to publish the bull without the approval of the king and his council.

'Because the pope ordered it,' replied Courtenay.

'Then choose between suffering confiscation of your temporalities and recalling your words with your own mouth,' retorted the Chancellor.

Courtenay felt that discretion was the better part of valour and recalled the interdict by proxy. England would go this far in her conflict with Rome, but a complete break with the pontiff would have to wait until she had grown stronger and the papacy weaker.

But what of the actual bulls and their effectiveness? When the papal letters were signed, Edward III was still alive but ten days later the crown passed to Richard II. Apart from the fact that the bull had been sent to his grandfather and not to Richard, matters like this were pushed to one side in the excitement that followed his accession to the throne, his coronation and the festivities that followed. When these had died down and the Commons met in October 1377, they renewed the policy of the Good Parliament: in other words, they took a strong anti-papal stand.

At this time Wycliffe even appeared before Parliament in person and gave the members a defence of his alleged heresies. But when one reads this, it is in such technical language that one doubts if many of the knights of the shire, who made up the Lower House, really understood him. But one fact is clear, they were all on Wycliffe's side and firmly against Rome.

It is most remarkable that a man under the ban of the papal bulls should be so bold. The Commons actually asked Wycliffe for his opinion on the important matter then being debated. It concerned the question of withholding payment of taxes to the pontiff. Can 'the kingdom of England lawfully, in case of necessity, detain and keep back the treasures of the kingdom for its own defence, that it be not carried away to foreign and strange nations, the pope himself demanding and requiring the same, under pain of censure, and by virtue of obedience?', they asked.

Wycliffe gave an unhesitating and dogmatic reply. For a start, England was at war and desperately short of money.

Charity begins at home, declared Wycliffe, and therefore it would not be charity but rank stupidity to send alms from England when the realm needed them urgently. Like Luther after him, Wycliffe attached little importance to the decisions of canon law or even civil law on this matter. Instead he appealed to 'the principles of the law of Christ'.

Some years before, Wycliffe had propounded a theory on lordship or dominion. In his tracts on this he stated that lordship (in any sphere) could only be possessed and exercised by the righteous man, the person who enjoyed God's grace. This person was truly a 'lord of the whole universe' but, just as Christ had shared everything with his followers, so this righteous man must have all things in common with other Christians. By contrast, the unrighteous man, who was not in a state of grace, thereby forfeited his claim to authority and to material possessions.

It can be seen that, while such a theory could safely be debated in the halls of Oxford in the fourteenth century, it was capable of revolutionary interpretation elsewhere. Wycliffe had been careful to remind people that, because of sin, civil power was essential and there remained a place for private property, even that of the unrighteous.

This teaching on 'lordship' lay behind Wycliffe's reply to Parliament. Not only did the pope have no legal claims over endowments for the English church, but by his corrupt life he had forfeited any rights that he might once have possessed. He was the 'unrighteous man' mentioned in Wycliffe's writings.

In addition to his reply to Parliament, Wycliffe also used the opportunity to write a pamphlet explaining his views in more detail. 'Christ, the Head of the church, whom all Christian priests ought to follow, lived by the alms of devout women. He hungered and thirsted; he was a stranger, and many other miseries he sustained, not only in his members, but also in his own body, as the apostle witnesseth. He was made poor for our sakes, that through his poverty we might be rich.'

Wycliffe then expounded our Lord's teaching on 'the kings of the Gentiles lord it over them . . . But you are not to be like that' (Luke 22:25,26). 'Here, lordship and dominion is forbidden to the apostles, and darest thou then

Defiance of the pope

usurp the same? If thou wilt be a lord, thou shalt lose thine apostleship . . . So this, then, is the true form and institution of the apostles' trade; lordship and rule is forbidden, ministration and service commanded.'[1]

'Beware,' said Wycliffe, 'lest you injure your fathers in purgatory if you permit money paid for masses for the dead to be paid to the pope.' He then proceeded to expound his views on disendowment but when he reached this point in his statement before Parliament they curtly ordered him to be silent. They had heard enough. But the fact that he had been consulted at all while under the ban of the pope's bulls shows how popular many of his doctrines had become with England's temporal leaders.

From this it is easy to guess what action the prelates took. To quote one historian, 'They maintained a masterly inactivity.' They could see that the tide had turned against them and their popularity had dropped dramatically. They decided the best thing to do was to bide their time. For Courtenay this must have been specially painful as he still simmered with anger over his defeat at St Paul's.

Finally there was Oxford. This was Wycliffe's own university, but would they take action after they received the papal bull? For months the leaders at Oxford ignored the pope's letter. The bull from the Vatican ordered them to arrest Wycliffe or else lose all the privileges that Oxford held from the pope. At this time a strong party in favour of the reformer existed at the university, but quite apart from this the common law of England prohibited the arrest of a king's subject in obedience to a papal bull.

Then, six months later, in December, Sudbury and Courtenay began to stretch their claws a little, and ordered the Oxford authorities to arrest Wycliffe, as the pope had demanded. This put the leaders into an awkward position. A chronicler of the time records the method used to get out of the difficulty. Wycliffe consulted the leaders at Oxford and they agreed that 'they should not imprison a man of the King of England at the command of the pope, lest they should seem to give the pope lordship and regal power in England'.[2]

But, as it was necessary to make a gesture, the vice-chancellor ordered Wycliffe to stay in Black Hall and not go out. He agreed to do this and so helped the university to preserve its privileges. The Oxford leaders hoped by this collusion to satisfy both pope and Parliament. After consulting all the masters in theology the chancellor declared publicly that Wycliffe's condemned doctrines 'were true, though they sounded badly to the ear'.[3] Undoubtedly this year was the high-water mark of Wycliffe's general popularity in Oxford, as well as in England generally.

At this point it may well be asked whether Wycliffe was actually guilty of doctrinal heresies in the eyes of Rome, or was it in fact his political actions that had caused the pope to send these bulls? So far it has been observed that he was a loyal son of the church but one who certainly wanted reform in many places and who wished to see the pontiff's power curbed. But had his views changed doctrinally? It would appear that, while he had begun to change his teaching on some points as he studied the Scriptures, it was more his political actions that caused these accusations to be hurled at him. When Parliament had asked Wycliffe if it was lawful to withhold payment from the pope, his reply had been an unhesitating 'Yes'. This must have roused the papal fury to boiling-point.

In the bull sent to Sudbury and Courtenay, the pope had compared Wycliffe to 'Marsilius of Padua and John of Ganduno, both of cursed memory'. These men had been obliged to flee to the Emperor Lewis of Bavaria when they attacked the papacy. The writings of Marsilius not only laid the axe at the roots of papal supremacy, but also maintained the reformed doctrine of justification by grace alone. He declared that merits or works are not the cause of our salvation; they are the fruit of the born-again Christian. For this he was condemned by Pope John XXII in 1330.

The pontiff so greatly feared the doctrine of Marsilius that he ordered that the investigations be made with the utmost secrecy. If Wycliffe should confess these teachings then his confessions must be 'kept strictly concealed' and Wycliffe detained until the Vatican gave further orders. The pope even expressed fears for the 'defilement' of the king and the royal family by such 'pestilent perversions'. This revealed Rome's fear of the simple biblical truth that Christians are justified by faith alone.

Defiance of the pope

These fears were groundless. Careful investigation shows that only profound points of doctrine were involved. Wycliffe denied to the pope the power to bind and loose and declared that unjust excommunication had no real effect. But these, added to the points mentioned above, touched only minor points of doctrine and mainly posed a threat to the authority of Rome and her greed for money. Even Wycliffe's leanings towards presbyterianism presented a direct challenge to the power and authority believed to be held by one man. It required more time and careful searching of the Scriptures to enable Wycliffe to see clearly the fundamental doctrines of the Christian faith. When these became clear to him, his writings would lay an axe at the root of the papal tree.

It has been suggested by at least one historian that near the end of 1377 the possibility existed of true reformation within the English church. If only Lancaster had been wholeheartedly on Richard's side he might have continued his anti-clerical actions and, together with Wycliffe, he could have begun a reformation and anticipated Henry VIII. But in view of Wycliffe's slow doctrinal progress this is impossible. Until he discovered the basic doctrine of justification by faith, any reform could only have been in the outward trappings of the church. One has only to consider his recent remarks about purgatory to realize that he still had a long way to go.

Despite Oxford's lack of co-operation and the tactics employed to satisfy the papal bull, early in 1378 a synod was convened in Lambeth Palace and Wycliffe was ordered to appear before the bishops in April. John of Gaunt no longer ruled the council. How would Wycliffe defend himself now?

---

1. J. Foxe, *Acts and Monuments*, Vol. i, p. 584.
2. *Eulogium Historiarum*, Vol. iii, p. 348.
3. *Ibid.*

9.
Accused of heresy

1377–1379 (3)

The gold and silver robes of the clergy and the purple worn by Sudbury, Courtenay and other bishops contrasted with the grey stone walls of Lambeth Palace. Wycliffe's appearance rather matched the walls, with his simple black gown and full, flowing dark beard.

He had come in full confidence that God would stand by him, and the splendour of the dignitaries that surrounded him failed to overawe him. It is interesting to note that, for a man accused of such offences, Wycliffe had not been arrested and dragged as a prisoner to the palace; he had merely been summoned to appear before Sudbury. But, strange as it may seem, he now stood in a stronger position than he had done at St Paul's. Then, Sudbury and Courtenay had acted within the accepted rights of the English bishops. Now, after the arrival of Pope Gregory's bulls, they stood in a somewhat delicate position.

While it had not been spelled out, the bulls had raised the question of King John and papal jurisdiction in England. No one, except the bishops, would admit this. But with the knowledge that last year even Parliament had asked Wycliffe for his advice, the bishops knew that they would have to tread carefully. The papal bulls might make the faithful tremble at Rome, but here, hundreds of miles away, they were just pieces of parchment which the barons could toss to one side if they so wished.

Memories of St Paul's must have passed through the minds of Sudbury and Courtenay as they waited for the trial to begin. To be sure, John of Gaunt and Lord Percy were not there; their power was largely gone. But all round the palace they could hear the cries of the people of London. They, too, had changed and were no longer on the bishops' side.

Just before the trial began, Sir Lewis Clifford entered the court with a message from the queen mother, the Black Prince's widow. The dowager queen forbad them to take any definite action against Wycliffe. The trial could proceed — the queen would permit this — but, no matter what its result and findings, their hands were absolutely tied. The trial would in fact be a mere farce.

The message made the papal commissioners' hearts sink. Even if they found Wycliffe guilty, they could not send him to Rome. As Walsingham records, though they were vested with all the authority of the apostolic see, they became 'shaken as a reed with the wind, became as soft as oil in their speech, to the open forfeiture of their own dignity, and the injury of the whole church'.

It was easy enough for Walsingham, the monastic chronicler, to abuse Courtenay as a mere 'time-server'. But he was writing in the safety of a monastery at St Albans. Courtenay had to face all England — nobles, merchants, yeomen and peasants.

Despite the orders from the dowager queen, the prelates went ahead cautiously with the trial. Before this took place they had sent Wycliffe a list of the heresies or errors that they believed he had propagated. John had carefully prepared a document giving his answers to their charges.

It is impossible in the space available to follow all the nineteen charges of heresy and Wycliffe's replies to these, but certain important points stand out in his answers. They show, too, Wycliffe's growth in understanding of the heresies present in the Roman church.

The pope has no political dominion, Wycliffe maintained, his power is spiritual only and God is his Judge. He has no supremacy even over the temporal goods of the clergy. As for the 'binding and loosing' or the 'power of the keys', this is only ministerial; it cannot keep anyone from the kingdom of heaven. Absolution counts for nothing unless God has first forgiven the sinner. As for excommunication, it cannot hurt anyone unless that person has first excommunicated himself from God by sin.

The pope, Wycliffe declared, is not above the church. He is capable of sinning and if 'the whole college of cardinals is remiss in correcting him for the necessary welfare of the church, it is evident that the rest of the body, which, as it may chance, may chiefly be made up of the laity, may medicinally reprove him . . . and reduce him to live a better life' (Article XVIII).

At some point during the trial the one thing that the prelates feared most took place — the mob burst into the Lambeth Chapel. The final blow had fallen. The bishops grew pale and looked at one another in despair as a number of Londoners, including many wealthy merchants, marched in and announced their support for Wycliffe and his teaching. 'In this way', records Walsingham, a staunch Romanist, 'that slippery John Wycliffe deluded his inquisitors, mocked the bishops, and escaped them by the favour and care of the Londoners, although all his propositions are clearly heretical and depraved.'

John did not leave the matter there. While he was permitted to return in safety to Oxford after being ordered by the papal commissioners to stop teaching these things 'on account of the scandal which they excited among the laity', he had more to say. For a start, he ignored the order to stop teaching: that continued. But he realized that despite the restraint of the court by the dowager queen, no one would restrain the pontiff when he learned of the court's findings. His time was surely running out.

In a second paper he expanded his answers to the papal delegates and grew even bolder in his speech. If he had but a short time to live, then the more people who knew of his teaching, the better. When writing about the pope, the words 'Antichrist', 'Lucifer' and 'Man of Sin' were used unhesitatingly. 'But a prohibition of reading of the sacred Scriptures and a vanity of secular dominion and a lusting after worldly appearances would seem to partake too much of a disposition towards the blasphemous advancement of Antichrist, especially while the truths of a scriptural faith are reputed "tares", and said to be opposed to the Christian truth.'

1378 was not only the point of no return in Wycliffe's public career; it also became the crossroads in his theological life. As one modern historian says, 'He stepped firmly from the orthodoxy of the day into heresy.' John had also entered the third phase of his life. His main concern now was sound theology and, very soon, making this known to the men and women of England.

The very words 'prohibition of reading of the sacred Scriptures' in his second paper suggest that he was clearly thinking of a wider audience than the students at Oxford. Was he, in fact, meditating on a translation of the Bible for the people of England?

He need not have feared Gregory XI's power. That pope died before any action could be taken and the confusion that followed the elections at Rome took the spotlight off England and Wycliffe. Surely God had timed this.

Since Wycliffe was at the height of his popularity, the government did not let the question of John and the Oxford authorities rest there. Even though John had himself agreed to stay in Black Hall on the vice-chancellor's orders, technically, the chancellor was guilty of imprisoning one of the king's subjects and obeying the pontiff. Already ill-feeling existed between the vice-chancellor and the government. The next thing he knew, he had been arrested and thrown into prison. The English Parliament would have no truck with anything that carried an odour of the papal Inquisition, which had been created about a hundred and fifty years before this to deal with heretics.

Wycliffe, as has been noted, was then in his heyday, but even after his death, and in the following century, England stood more or less alone in her method of dealing with heretics. The church and state bestowed upon them some very cruel punishment, but still the Inquisitors must have felt frustrated since they were barred from England. To be sure, persecution is a terrible thing in any time or place (and it was especially so in the Middle Ages) but the Inquisition was not merely a name, but a hideous weapon for evil used by the papacy. It had destroyed many in the past and was even now torturing the Waldenses (followers of Peter Waldo in France, who condemned the mass and the papacy and held that the Bible was the final authority in all spiritual questions). If the Inquisitors had been allowed to enter England, Wycliffe's story and England's history would have been very different.

At the very time that Wycliffe faced his accusers at Lambeth, the power that controlled the Inquisition had lost its leader. Pope Gregory XI had died and a momentous congress met at Rome. While this will be dealt with in more detail in the next chapter, it will be sufficient to say that a sharp division of opinion existed in the conclave of cardinals that met to elect a new pope. Many demanded a Roman; they wanted no more French pontiffs. Finally, after much arguing, an Italian, Urban VI, was elected. This tactless man soon lost favour with most of the cardinals and they retaliated by declaring his election void and then elected Clement VII. This new pope returned to Avignon and so began the 'Great Schism', with one pope at Avignon and one at Rome.

Wycliffe soon found himself involved in a political/ecclesiastical quarrel. During the Middle Ages, the church had long been the place of refuge for criminals and debtors. The 'sanctuary of holy church', as it was called, had become a veritable Cave of Adullam. Westminster was especially popular: the phrase 'take Westminster' being often on the lips of the creditor or criminal. Debtors took their goods and money to sacred ground and there they lived until their creditors' patience had expired or they themselves could escape overseas. Debtors were one thing, but murderers and thieves got exactly the same protection from justice. This often roused both the justices and the ordinary people to fury.

'Sanctuary' was a privilege of mixed value. It had been introduced by the church in the days of rough justice on the basis of Deuteronomy 19:2—13: 'One who kills his neighbour unintentionally without malice aforethought ... may flee to one of these cities and save his life' (Deuteronomy 19:4,5). It was intended by the church that the person guilty of a crime should avoid execution by hurrying to a church or other consecrated ground and then have the chance to leave the country within forty days. As the innocent could often suffer before the case had been properly investigated, this was commendable, but more often than not, deliberate criminals abused the privilege.

During the Spanish campaign, in 1367, two English knights, Shakell and Haule, had captured a Spanish count.

Later they released him in return for his own son, while the count returned to Spain to raise the large sum demanded as a ransom for the boy. Ten years later, they were still waiting for the ransom money. When Richard ascended the throne the possession of so important a hostage became a delicate matter. Parliament sent for the boy, but the knights refused to release him. They insisted on their right to the ransom money. Shakell and Haule were sent to the Tower and stayed there for over a year. One night they escaped, injuring the jailor *en route*, and fled to Westminster Abbey where they lived 'in sanctuary' among the monks. They hoped that either times would change or that they might escape and take the young Spaniard with them.

In August 1378, the Governor of the Tower came with Lord Latimer and a number of knights and demanded that the two criminals should be handed over. Shakell they soon arrested but Haule was attending mass at the time. The soldiers attempted to arrest him but a fight broke out. Haule bravely drew his sword but, after being chased twice round the choir, was stabbed to death. A church attendant was also killed and Haule's body dragged to the abbey door.

Sudbury excommunicated the governor, all his soldiers and everyone who had aided and abetted him. But the king and Parliament stood firmly with the governor. While the government regretted the murder, they maintained the right of civil officers to arrest those guilty of crime, even on church premises. Richard ordered the reading of excommunication to cease and said that the abbey must be reconsecrated.

Here they reached an impasse. The Abbot of Westminster, supported by all the bishops, refused to allow this and services at Westminster ceased for a time. Courtenay, true to form, read the excommunication at St Paul's Cross in defiance of the king and sought to stir up ill-feeling against Gaunt. An open quarrel now followed between church and state. Parliament even met in Gloucester that October, not only because of the 'cold war' but also because the abbey (which was normally used by Parliament) was unconsecrated and the abbot and monks still defied them.

The parliament which met in Gloucester debated at

length the question of its right to arrest a man in a church. The whole question of sanctuary was discussed and the government reaffirmed its right to make such arrests. Sanctuary had become a public nuisance and must be corrected. Too many criminals fled to the nearest church or abbey and escaped from justice. In the days long before criminal detectives had been even thought of, felons could often escape by night to some other part of England. They need not even go overseas.

John of Gaunt had intended to raise this question but for once Sudbury anticipated him and complained on behalf of the church. In the ensuing debate, various doctors of theology and civil law were called on behalf of the king. One of the former was John Wycliffe, who read a paper which has been preserved.

Wycliffe's paper reveals that Lancaster had led the attack on this ecclesiastical privilege. While Wycliffe declared that he could not attempt to defend the murder of Haule, he maintained the right of officers of law to enter the sanctuary to arrest the man. John tried to prove that sanctuary was illegal.

As we might expect, Wycliffe began his arguments by turning to the Scriptures. God, he claimed, gave the Israelites the cities of refuge for accidental homicide, not for deliberate murder. Sanctuary was a defiance of justice and without this, the state could not survive. The way that debtors and murderers pleaded mercy was pure hypocrisy. To rob a creditor of his money or take a person's life was not mercy. The clergy never forgave people who failed to pay the debts owed to them, so why should the state?

The final result was a very mild statute, passed in the spring of 1379, that left the problem virtually untouched. 'The most absurd legislative mouse' is the way that G. M. Trevelyan describes it. This statute disgusted Wycliffe, especially when he found that it had reconciled the church and state. He prepared a pamphlet, *De Officio Regis*, which was later woven into a longer work of his.

The church, claimed Wycliffe, should come under the supervision of the secular power, as she had proved unable to reform herself. Popes, cardinals and bishops refused to reform themselves or deal with the glaring evils in the church.

Accused of heresy

The only answer that Wycliffe could see was for the state to step in and act as guardian. The bishops should be made to investigate the state of the clergy in their diocese and all immoral or inefficient men should be removed. The king should make certain that there were no absentee clerics and all clergy should be made to study. There must be no ignorant priests.

This theory is called Erastianism, control of the church by the state. Strangely enough, the English Reformation later took this form under the Tudors and Stuarts. Wycliffe evidently hoped that some kind of reform would take place, especially after the loud protests that he heard raised against the church at the Gloucester Parliament.

Soon, however, the heat died down and church and state became once more reconciled. Wycliffe's hopes for success vanished but all his life he continued to hold this Erastian doctrine of the church. While this theory is most certainly not scriptural, it sounded blasphemous to the ears of any medieval churchman. Alongside this revolutionary theory, Wycliffe laid another. The hierarchy of his day taught that the ecclesiastical organization should be international. Hence the large number of Italians and Frenchmen that held English benefices. Wycliffe insisted that England should have an English church, governed by Englishmen, even though the king and the state were to be at its head. No foreigners should have any part in it.

During the year 1379, while at Oxford, Wycliffe became dangerously ill. Overwork, increasing age and, above all, the strain brought about by his recent trial, had weakened him. He did not have a very strong constitution and his old enemies, the friars, thought that he was about to die. They hoped that on his deathbed the heretic would recant and deny at least some of his heresies.

A deputation, composed of one from each of the mendicant orders, together with four aldermen from the city, came to his bedside. They reminded him of the grievous wrongs he had committed by teaching these heresies and threatened him with the judgement of heaven.

To their surprise they found him quiet and serene. He listened to their words and then asked his servant to raise him up on the bed. Although pale and weak, he turned and faced them boldly as they waited for his recantation.

'I shall not die, but live,' he asserted in a firm voice, 'and again declare the evil deeds of the friars.'

The friars looked at one another in astonishment and left the room in confusion. John's words were prophetic. The Lord laid his healing hand upon him and restored Wycliffe to fulfil his words.

Wycliffe's Bible

The beginning of Mark's Gospel from the translation by Wycliffe

10.
Forbidden book

1379–1381

The Great Schism of the papacy (1378–1417) is one of the blots on the history of the Roman Catholic Church that the majority of its members would like to erase. Nevertheless, it remains a historical fact that cannot be ignored. Apart from the service that it rendered Wycliffe by taking the spotlight off England and away from him, it served as an excellent object lesson in later years to men like Luther. He could look at it and see clearly that a church that could be divided for so long, for such trifling reasons, with popes condemning and excommunicating one another, could not possibly be all that it claimed. What, for example, of the dogma that the church must be visibly one?

There had been rival popes before but the Great Schism had this difference: previously, rival popes had been chosen by rival parties, but here Urban VI, the first pope chosen, had been elected by all the cardinals present. The cardinals might later protest that they had chosen Urban under pressure, but the fact remained that they had accepted his rule as supreme pontiff for several months and they had not murmured, so this cut little ice with any intelligent man.

If there had been a major doctrinal difference between Avignon and Rome, such as divided the Roman church from the Greek church, this could have been understood to some extent by the more discerning layman. But in this case it was mainly a question of personality.

At the election, eleven of the sixteen cardinals present were French, but all had unanimously voted for the Archbishop of Bari as Urban VI. One of the big mistakes that Urban made was speedily to commence some much needed reform. He began with a reduction in the income of the cardinals and they did not like it. Wage cuts have never been popular!

Another big difference, however, existed between Urban and his cardinals. Apart from his tactlessness, he held strong ideas about his power and authority, while the cardinals held to the more traditional view that they, as a body, should curb, and to some extent control, any papal autocracy. In the fourteenth century the teaching on the supremacy, infallibility and power of the pope differed from what is now claimed by him.

This clash caused the eleven French cardinals to protest that Urban had only been elected (through their votes) under pressure from the Roman crowds. They moved to Fondi four months after the election, declared Urban's election void, and elected Cardinal Robert of Geneva as Clement VII. Shortly after this he settled down in Avignon.

Urban VI created twenty-eight new cardinals to bring his court up to strength and both pontiffs remained adamant. Soon, the countries of Europe chose either Rome or Avignon and rallied round the pontiff of their choice. England, much of Germany, Hungary, Bohemia and Scandinavia supported Urban, as did northern and central Italy. France, Spain, Scotland, Naples, Sicily and some parts of Germany chose Clement. Europe was pained and shocked. While it groaned under the increased taxation necessary to support two papal courts, popular regard for the papacy dropped dramatically.

At first Wycliffe greeted the new Roman pontiff warmly as one who would break the evils of Avignon. He had high hopes of one who might bring reform. These hopes were soon dashed to the ground, especially when it became clear that Urban VI claimed so much power and authority and would not permit the cardinals to limit it in any way.

When Wycliffe saw this he wrote another treatise, *Schisma Papae* ('the Schism of the Popes'), in which he invited the sovereigns of Europe to seize their opportunity and shake off all Roman dominion. 'Trust we in the help of Christ,' he declared, 'for he hath begun already to help us graciously, in that he hath cloven the head of Antichrist, and made the two parts fight against each other; for it cannot be doubtful

Forbidden book

that the sin of the popes, which hath so long continued, hath brought in the division.'

Now was the time, Wycliffe declared, for kings and emperors to unite and 'recover the heritage of the church and to destroy the foul sins of clerks . . . Thus should peace be established, and simony destroyed.' 'Of all heresies, none could be greater than the belief that a man may be absolved from sin, if he give money, or because a priest layeth his hand on the head, and saith, "I absolve thee." Thou must be sorrowful in thy heart, or God absolveth thee not.' Wycliffe then denied the need for confession to a priest. Even in a treatise on the Great Schism, Wycliffe wrote of the personal walk of the Christian and the unbiblical teaching on absolution insisted upon by Rome. This shows how John's theology was becoming more biblical. This may not appear so startling to the average reader, but to people in the fourteenth century it was revolutionary. It reveals how Wycliffe's mind was shaking off the medieval trappings. Unfortunately the kings of Europe failed to respond.

Shortly before this Wycliffe had published another work, *On the Truth of Holy Scripture.* In this he contended for the supreme authority and entire sufficiency of the Scriptures and for the need to translate them into English. Other opponents of the pope had appealed to the Bible as the ultimate authority in all cases of argument in doctrinal matters, but Wycliffe went further. He insisted on the right of every Christian to study and know the Bible for himself. Each Christian had the right to private judgement and, since Scripture alone was sufficient for salvation, canon law, pilgrimages, fasts, prayers to saints and the mass were all either unnecessary or unscriptural.

This was an outstanding work and, for those days, even more revolutionary in its views than his treatise on the papal schism. If you failed to know the Bible, Wycliffe argued, then you could not know Christ; but if you read it in faith and asked the Holy Spirit for guidance, it could be understood. When you came to a passage that was incomprehensible, the fault lay with you, not with the Bible. Unlike the Scholastic theologians who claimed that each portion of Scripture had three, mainly allegorical meanings, Wycliffe claimed that each passage (apart from the poetic ones) should be taken literally — although he did concede that a spiritual meaning could be concealed behind it.

This was 'cutting the Gordian knot'. For centuries most of the few people who read the Bible failed to understand it because of the Scholastic teaching. From now on any who read or heard the Bible could take the words seriously in their literal sense, once they had read Wycliffe's treatise.

It is only logical to assume that when he wrote these words, Wycliffe was planning a translation of the Bible into English. For several centuries French translations had existed and these were used, in a limited way, by some of the nobility and upper classes. Wycliffe complained with much justification, 'As the lords of England have the Bible in French, so it would not be against reason that they [the peasants and yeomen] should have the same words in English.'

Wycliffe had found from hard experience that the only true guide for man was God's Word. It had become his touchstone for everything, most of all for matters relating to the spiritual and moral life. As he had found it indispensable, how could the ordinary people manage without it?

The Bible then available to the priests in a very limited way, since printing had not been invented, was the Latin translation produced by Jerome between A.D. 383 and 405. This came to be known as the Latin Vulgate and was without doubt the version used by Wycliffe himself. But Latin meant little or nothing to the ordinary layman, so Wycliffe declared he must have an English translation.

It would appear that at this stage of his life (1378–1380), the translation was still only an idea in his mind. One historian (G. M. Trevelyan) has described these years as 'the years of germination, not action'. During this time Wycliffe thought about his plans for a translation until the day came when he was ready to act.

At this point it is only right to ask, 'Did we ever have a complete Bible in English in any of its stages from Old English (which was spoken after the Anglo-Saxon invasion) to Middle English (c. 1100–1500)?' (Modern English dates from 1500 onwards.) Unfortunately, the most careful search of history indicates that we did not.

Aldhelm, the first Bishop of Sherbourne, Dorset, is said

to have translated the Psalms into Old English about A.D. 700. While the Venerable Bede wrote mostly in Latin, his disciple, Cuthbert, stated that Bede was translating John's Gospel when he died. But no trace of this translation has survived.

To turn from the clergy to royalty, it is known that King Alfred of Wessex (871–901) either translated, or ordered to be translated, some of Bede's work into English. Later he published a code of laws and prefaced this with the Ten Commandments in English, with extracts from Exodus 21–23. These were followed by an extract from Acts 15: 23–29. He is also said to have translated part of the Psalter into English.

Apart from interlinear 'glosses' written into Latin manuscripts, the only extant Old English version of the Gospels is that known as the Wessex Gospels, dating from about the ninth or tenth century. Near the end of the tenth century, Abbot Aelfric of Eynsham translated parts of the first seven books of the Old Testament.

But William and the Norman Conquest of 1066 struck a heavy blow to English culture and such literature as we then possessed. The Normans spoke French and this caused English to change radically, so much so that, after a generation or two, the few Old English versions of the Bible that existed would have become unintelligible to the majority of people.

From this time on, until Wycliffe began his work, the only type of translations made were stories of Genesis and Exodus, which appeared in rhyming English verse, and both metrical and prose versions of the Psalms.

This brief survey has not mentioned the change in the teaching of the Roman church concerning the reading of Scripture by the layman. This took place gradually through the centuries but it largely explains the absence of translations, apart from the poor education of many of the clergy and the shortage of books. 'Where there is a will, there is a way,' and if they had been convinced that the Bible should be made available in the national or local language, doubtless the more scholarly would have made a translation available to the people.

But while the traditional teaching of the church had

become increasingly opposed to laymen reading the Bible, the Council of Valencia (1229) officially forbad them to read 'the books of the Old and New Testament, unless anyone should wish, from a feeling of devotion, to have a psalter or breviary for divine service, or the hours of the blessed Mary. But we strictly forbid them to have the above-mentioned books in the vulgar tongue.'[1] At the Reformation, the Council of Trent reaffirmed this decree.

Some may ask, 'Why did Rome forbid the reading of the Bible?' The answer is simple. Apart from the superstitious way that the hierarchy themselves regarded God's Word, they knew that its teaching struck at the very foundation of their power. If this were known by the layman, their edifice would fall. Take but one verse: 'It is for freedom that Christ has set us free. Stand firm, then, and do not let yourselves be burdened again by a yoke of slavery' (Galatians 5:1). Teaching such as this could have brought down the whole hierarchy of the pope, cardinals, bishops and priests.

These considerations give some idea of the obstacles that Wycliffe faced: not only a lack of Hebrew and Greek manuscripts, lexicons, dictionaries and other books to assist him, but the opposition of the entire church. Translating the Bible is a daunting task, even in ideal conditions, with every manuscript and book that is needed to assist the translator, and when one is working in close collaboration with others. To tackle such a task on one's own, without these modern essentials, and with opposition from the whole church, is a labour of Herculean proportions. Small wonder that Wycliffe needed time to consider and plan the work over those years 1378–1380.

But while Wycliffe needed time to think deeply about a translation of the Bible, these were certainly not idle years. Other important subjects had to be thought through and written about. Having faced numerous attacks from the body of people who called themselves 'the church', Wycliffe wrote in 1378 a treatise on *De Ecclesia* (The Church). In this he clearly distinguished between those who appeared to be members of the church militant and those who were true members, not only of the church here on earth, but who would also one day dwell with Christ in eternity. He did this with one sweeping stroke by taking up Paul's

Forbidden book

teaching on election. From pope to peasant, Wycliffe declared, no one could enter heaven or know salvation unless he was elect, that is, predestined to eternal life by the grace of God.

This teaching of Paul's had been set out in a logical form by Augustine, Bishop of Hippo (354—430). This doctrine had in some measure been officially accepted by much of the church at the time, but as the church became increasingly apostate, the teaching had become conveniently buried, just like the Bible. Rome lapsed into what is called 'semi-Pelagianism'.

Thomas Bradwardine, Wycliffe's spiritual father, brought this great biblical truth to light once more, emphasizing the sovereignty and grace of God. Unfortunately, he died in the Black Death in 1349 and left young Wycliffe to take up the torch at a later date and expound the doctrine clearly.

It may be asked, 'Why did such teaching become forgotten?' The answer to this is to look at the claims of Rome 'to bind and loose' and at the so-called 'power of the keys'. People who believed Rome's doctrine were truly 'bound'; they were in fact slaves to all Roman dogma and believed the papal claim that 'Outside the church, there is no salvation'. But those who believed the doctrine of election that Bradwardine and Wycliffe rediscovered could shake off the power of priest and confessional, once they knew that they had eternal life through Christ. They were, as Paul tells us, 'God's chosen people' (Colossians 3:12), and all the hierarchy were powerless against them. The twin truths of justification by faith and the Christian's election by God to eternal life were the rocks that were to shatter the power of Rome in the Reformation. Already in Wycliffe's time his teaching on election caused the pope and his hierarchy many sleepless nights and much anxiety.

When it is recognized that the church had been turning increasingly to sacraments, rituals, ceremony and pilgrimages to so-called 'holy places', it can be seen how the power of the church consisted in its ability to give or withhold the sacraments. As she taught that these were an essential means of grace, which assisted one to attain salvation, they were eagerly sought by the laity, and this gave the priests their power.

But as Professor Gotthard Lechler says, there 'runs like a scarlet thread through the whole system of Wycliffe's thinking . . . the thought that the Church is nothing else than *the whole number of the elect* . . . The Church, therefore, has in the visible world only its manifestation, its temporary pilgrimage; it has its home and its origin, as also its end, in the invisible world, in eternity. Every individual devout Christian owes all that he possesses in his inner life to the regeneration which is the fruit of election.'[2] By bringing this truth to light again, Wycliffe deserves to be called the grandfather of the Reformation, since Luther and Calvin have been named as its fathers.

Pope Boniface VIII had claimed that he was the head of the church. No, replied Wycliffe, Christ is the only Head of the church. While election and predestination decided who entered heaven, Wycliffe declared that true love and obedience to God's law in Christ were essential for the church on earth. He maintained that a man's actions, and not his doctrine, were the best test of whether he was a true Christian or not.

Obviously, teaching such as this aroused great anger from the hierarchy, but others had attacked papal power before. Wycliffe, however, attacked it in a different way, especially in his teaching on election. Rome taught that no person could enter heaven without the work of the priest. Wycliffe taught that laymen or priests, if they were true Christians, could come directly to God through Christ. A mediating priest was unnecessary, since all had a great High Priest in Christ. By this he implied the doctrine of the priesthood of all believers.

But Wycliffe's next major work rocked the papal edifice to its foundations. In 1379 and 1380 he lectured and wrote *On Apostasy* and *On the Eucharist.* His teaching on the latter was the bomb that rocked the papacy. Rome lays so much stress on the Eucharist and the mass (called by Protestants 'the Lord's Supper' or 'Holy Communion') that her priestly power can be said to centre on this, especially on the mass.

The early church had observed this ordinance as described in the Gospels and 1 Corinthians 11, in the simplest way. As our Lord said, 'Do this in remembrance of me' (1 Corinthians 11:24). But as the centuries passed and the ministers began to call themselves 'priests', the teaching about this had changed. As Dr Boettner has said, 'A priest without a sacrifice is simply no priest at all.'

To remedy this, and because of the increasing superstition and ignorance of priest and layman alike, the church invented a new kind of 'sacrifice'. Rome claimed that at the sacrifice of the mass, 'The Roman priest becomes an *"Alter Christus"*, that is, "Another Christ", in that he sacrifices the real Christ upon the altar and presents Him for the salvation of the faithful and deliverance of souls in purgatory.'[3]

How is this done? By means of his so-called priestly power, he changes the elements of bread and wine into the literal, physical body and blood of Christ. This is called 'transubstantiation' (a change of substance). The Creed of Pius IV states, 'That in the Mass is offered to God a true, proper and propitiatory sacrifice for the living and the dead; and that in the most holy sacrament of the Eucharist there is truly, really, and substantially, the body and blood, together with the soul and divinity, of our Lord Jesus Christ; and that there is a conversion of the whole substance of the bread into the body, and of the whole substance of the wine into the blood, which the Catholic Church calls Transubstantiation.'

This doctrine had not been accepted by the church in Britain in Anglo-Saxon times. In the tenth century, Aelfric, Abbot of St Albans, had declared, 'The host is the body of Christ, not bodily, but spiritually.' But then came the Norman Conquest and with the Normans came new bishops, including Lanfranc, the Archbishop of Canterbury. Not only was he a devoted supporter of the papacy, but he also claimed that, at the words of the priest, Christ left heaven and descended to the altar. In 1215 the doctrine of transubstantiation was formally accepted by the Fourth Lateran Council and from then on it had been universally accepted by the Western church. Now came Wycliffe's bombshell. He denied the doctrine completely and denounced it as idolatrous and the cause of priestly arrogance. It was unsupported by Scripture and early church tradition. It was also opposed to the testimony of the senses. Could not the bread or wafer and wine on the altar be seen to remain unchanged? Never, declared Wycliffe, had a heresy been more cunningly smuggled into the church than transubstantiation. It was 'a blasphemous deceit' and 'a veritable abomination of desolation in the holy places'.

When he wrote *On the Eucharist*, Wycliffe clearly became a heretic to the fourteenth-century church leaders. Anyone who denied the teaching on the mass was beyond the pale. His previous writings had edged close to heresy, perhaps in some cases were slightly heretical. But they were surrounded by so much philosophy that it was not easy for the hierarchy to see through the smoke-screen. Now in his teaching on the mass, he spoke in a clear enough manner.

Not only was the hierarchy furious at Wycliffe's teaching, but influential friends like Lancaster could not agree with him and follow him down this new path. John stood almost alone, with just a group of his followers at Oxford. He remained firm; he would not yield. In his lectures of 1381 he declared, 'The consecrated host we see upon the altar, is neither Christ, nor any part of him, but an effectual sign of him; and that transubstantiation, identification or impanation rest upon no scriptural ground.' Wycliffe held to the same doctrine as did Luther, that known as consubstantiation.

Doubtless Wycliffe had for some time spoken against this doctrine in his sermons, but when, from the chair of theology, he began a formal attack on this teaching, it soon reached the ears of the friars. They took this as a declaration of war. In 1381, he put forward twelve conclusions in his lectures, in which he utterly denied the official teaching of the church on transubstantiation.

An assembly of twelve doctors, eight of whom were monks or friars, met with the Chancellor, William de Berton. A decree was pronounced which declared Wycliffe's doctrine to be erroneous and repugnant to the church's teaching. It concluded by threatening imprisonment, suspension from scholastic teaching and the greater excommunication for any who taught or listened to Wycliffe's doctrine.

John was seated in his doctoral chair teaching this very subject when the doors burst open and the university officers entered and read the condemnation. He hesitated for a moment. His mind must have raced: 'Shall I abandon this

Forbidden book

truth to save my life?' 'Would it be expedient to recant — even to gain time?' But truth and courage prevailed in his heart and mind and he still stood firm.

His next action caused great astonishment. Wycliffe appealed to the king. People were accustomed to priests appealing to the bishop or even to the pope, but to appeal to the king over a 'spiritual' matter appeared outrageous. His boldness was too much for John of Gaunt, who forbad him to speak any further on this matter.

'I appeal to the king and the Parliament,' reasserted Wycliffe as he vacated his professorial chair.

1. L. Boettner, *Roman Catholicism*, p. 97.
2. G. Lechler, *John Wycliffe and his English Precursors* (translated by Professor Lorimer), R.T.S., pp. 288–290.
3. L. Boettner, *Roman Catholicism*, p. 174.

11.
Preaching the Word

1381–1382 (1)

It is impossible to say precisely when Wycliffe's first band of preachers set off to evangelize parts of England. The reformer had now openly affirmed that every man had the right to study and know the Bible for himself. But while he meditated on the best way to begin an English translation, what better way to bring portions of the Bible to people than by other preachers?

He had, of course, New Testament precedent for this. Not only the apostles, but 'those who had been scattered preached the word wherever they went' (Acts 8:4). But Wycliffe had more recent examples of roving preachers. The mendicant friars, now his worst enemies, had been travelling preachers since early in the thirteenth century. They used every opportunity to preach but, alas, they did not preach the gospel. They were intent only on drawing men closer to the pope and collecting money.

In addition to the friars, men called 'pardoners' prepared the way for Wycliffe's followers, as well as showing how the common people could be reached. Frequently these were laymen, officials licensed by the pope or bishop to sell indulgences round the country, and they often used religious relics to gain a hearing with the superstitious people. They were extremely unpopular with the clergy and friars, who bitterly opposed them, but as they bore papal authority, no one could forbid them. A pardoner did not have to be a cleric and it was a bitter cup indeed for a priest to see his pulpit occupied by a layman, preaching after a fashion and hawking his papal indulgences.

These men may have helped the idea to germinate in

Wycliffe's mind: why should he not organize and train men to go out as 'poor preachers'? He now entered the third phase of his ministry, that of training and sending out his own preachers. To begin with, there was probably little organization about the work. It was a spontaneous thing. People must hear the Word and John's enthusiasm rubbed off on to his followers, who became known as 'Lollards' or 'poor priests'. ('Lollard' is thought to originate from a Flemish word meaning 'to mumble' or 'to mutter'. It soon came to be synonymous with 'heretic'.)

These preachers went equipped with tracts and some handwritten portions of English Scripture to exhort, convince and persuade those who would listen. A definite date cannot be given but it was probably about 1379/1380. As one historian says, 'We have little or no knowledge of [Wycliffe's] followers before 1382, the year in which persecution began.'

These 'poor priests' set off barefoot, with staffs in their hands, dressed in coarse robes, living on alms and eating the simplest food. Wycliffe warned them not to copy the friars in other respects: 'Go and preach, it is the sublimest work; but imitate not the priests whom we see after the sermon sitting in the ale-house, or at the gaming-table . . . After your sermon is ended, do you visit the sick, the aged, the poor, the blind and the lame and succour them . . .'

One of the most eloquent and greatly loved of these men was John Aston, a fellow of Merton College, Oxford. He could be seen wandering over the heath or sitting by a cottage hearth. Whether preaching to a crowd in a churchyard, or speaking to one or two people in their home, he did it gladly. Nicholas Hereford, Philip Repton, Robert Alington and John Ashwardby are the other leading Oxford men who supported Wycliffe in this work.

In this way the light of the gospel began once more to spread in England, starting with Lutterworth, which was, of course, their main centre. Later other centres were formed, where groups of local people carried the Word to surrounding villages and hamlets.

While Wycliffe's 'poor preachers' were a new thing, Lollardy was not. There had been popular anti-clerical movements, both on the Continent and in England, for some time. These were composed of people who disliked the authority and priestcraft of Rome. We have little record of them, except for accounts of their trials and persecutions. They represented a stubborn trend of popular piety which existed outside the organized church and whose origins are lost in the mists of antiquity. The main tenets found in these movements (such as the Waldensians and Beghards) were teachings which differed sharply from that of the Catholic church on such subjects as the Eucharist, the pope, the Bible and the independence of the laity from the priests.

Wycliffe's teaching and preachers gave these people new life and his teaching thus often fell on receptive ears. Men who had sat at John's feet had their hearts and minds clearly focused on the essentials of the faith and when they went into the highways and byways of England, they sought to bring these clearly to their listeners.

But the Lollards soon roused the anger of the clergy — especially that of the friars. Unable to preach the gospel themselves and denying their pulpits to the 'poor preachers', the latter endeavoured to rouse the people against them. Frequently they failed, as a group of strong men would muster round the preacher in the market-place to protect him, since all were hungry to hear more of God's Word.

Wycliffe constantly reaffirmed that the first duty of the clergy was to preach. This, he said, was of more benefit to the people than any sacrament. He emphasized the centrality in any service of the pulpit and the sermon, so putting himself yet again in marked contrast to those who wanted the altar to be central. This also made Wycliffe the forerunner of the Puritans. Not only the sermon, but also its content mattered. His preachers were not to amuse and entertain people, as did the friars, but to call them to repentance and faith.

He had no use for saints and their canonization by Rome. He believed the legends of their lives to be mere fables. But he did not forbid prayers to saints as necessarily wrong. He took a moderate view of the Virgin Mary, not going as far as John Knox, who threw her image into the water. Instead Wycliffe held up her life as an example to all, especially to women. But he forbad people to pray to her.

Iconoclasm (the destruction of images) did not enter John's teaching. He did not demand the destruction of images in his reform. He said that they were there as a sign to help Christians, and should be treated as such.

Many are astounded when they learn that Wycliffe never abandoned the Catholic fiction of purgatory. But to be fair, his ideas about this progressed. For John purgatory was a state where the souls of the departed *sleep* or rest, in other words, an intermediate state between earth and heaven. In his opinion, all that could be done by the prayers of the faithful would in some vague way improve the condition of those in purgatory. He maintained that the prayers for the dead by the pious layman prevailed with God, while those of the worthless prelate did not. Although this has no biblical basis, it stands in stark contrast to the Roman teaching, which regards purgatory as a state where the departed soul goes to be purified by the fires of purgatory — a direct denial of the efficacy of Christ's cleansing blood.

When the preachers returned to Wycliffe they told him of their successes and failures and the opposition of the friars. One thing stood out clearly in Wycliffe's mind: the people needed a Bible in the vernacular. The most his preachers could do was teach them verses or short passages of Scripture to memorize.

That seed of an idea was growing in John's mind. The people *must* have a Bible in English. The Lollard preachers kept telling him of the eagerness with which people grasped the fragments of Scripture which they taught them. Perhaps his illness and the threat of persecution brought home to him the fact that time was running out. He could be struck down again or the hierarchy in their fury might imprison him. At any rate, it appears that by 1380 he and a small group of followers were planning the translation.

The problems Wycliffe faced have already been mentioned. He had no knowledge of Greek or Hebrew, but then who had in the fourteenth century? He was a good Latin scholar and Wycliffe was accustomed to translating from the Vulgate for use in his sermons. Why not shake the dust from off all this and translate it into English?

He not only loved the Bible, but also had a good grasp of its meaning, and certain keen Oxford men were already assisting him in the work of the Lollard preachers. Some of these men could assist him in this work, too. While the traditional view maintains that Wycliffe translated much of the Bible, aided by a few men such as Nicholas Hereford, it is perhaps more accurate to think of Wycliffe as 'chairman' of a board of translators. He carefully supervised the work, translated parts himself, and sought to ensure that the whole work read easily and accurately.

For over a hundred and fifty years men have debated whether Wycliffe translated the Bible completely or whether the work was the product of a team. As one Victorian writer remarks, 'It is scarcely to be imagined, that ... Wycliffe disdained to receive such assistance as he could procure. The labour must have been such as to overpower almost any single-handed strength ...' What is important is that Wycliffe had the vision. He organized the work, carefully superintended the translation, and was scrupulous about checking it before it was copied. To him goes the honour of being the first Englishman to produce a Bible in the vernacular for England.

Nicholas Hereford, Doctor of Divinity and Oxford canon, who was one of Wycliffe's leading translators, was interrupted in his work when he was summoned to appear before the Blackfriars Synod of 1382. When this occurred he had translated up to Baruch chapter 3 (in the Apocrypha, which comes in the Vulgate between Old and New Testaments).

This first translation appears to have been completed before Wycliffe's death. While this was a monumental work, it gives a very literal, stilted and at times incomprehensible, translation of the Vulgate. It is easy to criticize such work today, when the difficulties faced by Wycliffe and his team are hard to appreciate. For one thing, three main dialects existed in Middle English, and they had to make a choice which one to use.

Nothing daunted, Wycliffe and his friends began a major revision of the Bible. This, it appears, was mainly the work of John Purvey, Wycliffe's secretary at Lutterworth. It was not completed until about 1395, but when it appeared it was much freer in its translation and also more idiomatic than the first version. Purvey used Midland English (as did Chaucer for the *Canterbury Tales*), and this translation became known as the Lollard Bible.

Preaching the Word

One can see God's hand in the change in Wycliffe's circumstances. Had he not been forced to resign his chair at Oxford, would he ever have found time to translate and supervise the first translation and commence the second?

The English-speaking world owes an immense debt to John Wycliffe, the man raised up by God to meet its need. He inspired William Tyndale in the sixteenth century and Tyndale's translation became the foundation of the 1611 Authorized Version. For centuries people both sides of the Atlantic have turned to this when they wished to read the Word of God. Even today, with the modern translations available, many people still prefer to use the 1611 version. This fourth and final phase of Wycliffe's ministry undoubtedly produced our greatest heritage.

While printing, invented by the Chinese, had not yet reached Europe, Wycliffe had a number of scribes carefully copy from the finished work. It is difficult to realize how much effort went into this alone. Since over a hundred manuscripts still survive, despite the laws that once banned them, it is probable that hundreds more must have been destroyed by the hierarchy that feared God's Word. Of those that survive, many belonged to the rich and to the nobility. Even Anne of Bohemia, Richard II's first wife, owned a Wycliffite Bible.

While John had been forced to resign from his chair at Oxford, he was still free to use his pen and the Chancellor of Oxford had no power over him at Lutterworth. Another tract that appeared at this time was *The Wicket*, which dealt mainly with his teachings on the Eucharist. It was less theological than his other writings and more easily understood by the average man or woman. In fact it could be said that here he used the language which he used in the pulpit.

This tract and other writings and teachings, and especially his 'poor preachers', have been blamed for the Peasants' Revolt of 1381. This accusation has been shown by historians to be entirely unjustified. For one thing, the indictments against the rebels never accused them of heresy and when, later, the Lollards were also tried for teaching heretical doctrines, they were not accused of having any part in the revolt nor of inciting the peasants.

For years England had suffered defeat in war, terrible

losses in the Black Death and through famine, yet the government demanded still more taxes from the poor people. The poll-tax Parliament voted for in the autumn of 1380 was about a shilling (5p) a head. In practice this varied from fourpence (1½p) to a shilling (5p) for each labouring family. The money was collected but the king's council soon found that their so-called 'calculations' were mere guesswork; they would not have enough. The population of England had fallen dramatically but they had failed to recognize this.

After consultation, a second body of collectors went forth, armed with powers of imprisonment, carefully scrutinizing the lists of inhabitants of each town, village and hamlet, to collect money forcibly from any who had evaded the collectors before. But the average person thought that they had come to levy a new poll-tax.

This was the spark that ignited the gunpowder. The people had lived in poverty most or all of their lives and seen the money they paid squandered by an inefficient parliament or equally inefficient military leaders. They deeply distrusted the government and one reason for the revolt was to protest against the king's advisers. Protest is, in fact, one of the key-words to the rising. It was not communistic, although ideas that smacked of this did circulate among the common people.

In their innocence, these simple people believed that the boy-king Richard would sympathize with them and that he would understand their aspirations for liberty. Liberty was the other key-word; it was what they demanded. At this time less than half the people of England possessed the privileges which the Magna Carta had secured for every 'freeman'.

A high percentage of the peasants were still 'serfs' or 'villeins', that is, men personally bound to their lords, to whom they paid dues and owed services. A serf could not plead in court against his lord. His lips were sealed. Neither could he leave his farm or sell his land without permission. These were the marks of the serf, who was in a similar position to the negro slave before Wilberforce.

The insurrection appears to have started in Essex on 2 June 1381, and Kent followed a few days later. By 10 June the counties surrounding London were all in revolt and marching on London. It spread like a forest fire. Somerset rose on the nineteenth and Yorkshire followed on the twenty-third. The insurrection spread so easily not only because people were ready for it, but also because no police force or standing army existed. An expedition for France was waiting at Plymouth but its leaders failed to realize the gravity of the position. 'Fearful lest their voyage should be prevented . . . they heaved their anchor and with some difficulty left the harbour . . . and put to sea.'

A man named John Ball headed the rising. He planned to have all servile dues in England changed to a rent of fourpence (1½p) an acre. Some of his leaders demanded the disendowment of the church, which was a large landowner, the abolition of game laws and the free use of forests. Ball was a chaplain, priest and religious zealot who had for twenty years been agitating the country, attacking both church and state. Frequently Ball would 'preach' in the market-place on Sunday, just as people were coming from church. One of the questions he often asked was 'Are we not all descended from the same parents, Adam and Eve?'

This may have been the origin of the catchword used by the insurgents:

> When Adam delved and Eve span
> Who was then the gentleman?

When the peasants reached Maidstone, they released John Ball from the archbishop's prison, where he had been jailed for preaching against the hierarchy. He now took his place as leader of the uprising. The peasants received a warm welcome as they entered Canterbury on 10 June and the rebels burst into the cathedral, interrupted the singing at mass, and called on the monks to elect a new archbishop because, they claimed, Sudbury would soon die as a traitor.

Apprentices and some democratically minded aldermen flung wide the gates of London. The king, his mother, Archbishop Sudbury and some noblemen shut themselves in the Tower of London. The peasants then blockaded the Tower. They declared that they wanted the heads of Gaunt, Sudbury, Hales and certain other ministers. Murders had already taken place in several parts of England but, generally speaking, the killings were few in relation to the size of the rebel army. The number of killings was small compared to those in the French or Russian revolutions. Those put to death were normally lawyers, judges (such as the Chief Justice of England), abbots (the largest landowners) and others with whom the peasants had old scores to settle.

John of Gaunt topped their list. Four years previously, at Wycliffe's trial at St Paul's, the Savoy (Gaunt's palace) had only just been spared. Now as they entered London they shouted, 'To the Savoy, to the Savoy!' Peasants and prentices burst into the palace, tore out the rich furnishings and destroyed it. Men hacked furniture to pieces with axes and threw it into the River Thames. But the majority stole nothing. Gaunt and all his possessions were accursed and should therefore be destroyed, not stolen. Finally the palace went up in flames. It was fortunate for John of Gaunt that he was then in Scotland.

King Richard was advised to call a conference at Mile End, to the east of the City of London. The rebels agreed to this but only part of their army went there. The rest kept the Tower under siege. The young king went out, met the rebels and made specious promises which his counsellors certainly did not intend to keep. This dispersed many of the insurgents, who felt that they had achieved their purpose. Meanwhile other rebels had broken into the Tower, dragged out Sudbury, executed him on Tower Hill and stuck his head on London Bridge. This vindictiveness against him arose from the fact that he was Chancellor of England, and therefore directly connected with the taxation. His office as archbishop failed to protect him. A marked change of relations between church and people had taken place in the three hundred years since the death of Thomas à Becket.

Another conference took place at Smithfield, in the market-square. The rebels met there, led by Wat Tyler, and were faced by the young king and his supporters. A quarrel broke out in which Tyler was killed by Walworth, the Mayor of London. Richard acted wisely and courageously and the peasants dispersed without further bloodshed. Once they surrendered their hold on London, the rising was doomed.

A cruel reaction ensued, with bloody assizes which

mocked the pardons made by Richard. All promises made were broken, but the revolt probably hastened the emancipation which came partly in the fifteenth century and partly in Tudor days.

In the chaos that followed the rising, much confusion of facts also abounded. It is not surprising that Wycliffe and his preachers should be blamed for the Peasants' Revolt. Some of Wycliffe's teaching on lordship and even predestination could be twisted so that it appeared to challenge authority and even suggest anarchy. A few Lollards may have had some such ideas. Some monastic writers declared that the revolt was the judgement of heaven on the English hierarchy for failing to deal firmly with Wycliffe. Sudbury's death was even referred to as 'a needful expiation for the sinful laxity of his discipline'.

There would certainly be no such laxity in his successor. In October 1381, Bishop Courtenay was nominated as Archbishop of Canterbury. He was a born persecutor and cast in a totally different mould from Sudbury. What did the future hold for John and the Lollards?

12.
Persecution

1381–1382 (2)

Courtenay wasted no time. He had the natural instincts of a persecutor and succeeded Sudbury at the best possible time to use his powers to the full. At Wycliffe's trial at St Paul's, he had pushed himself to the fore, even in front of the archbishop, because persecution seemed to flow in his veins. The clergy blamed Sudbury for allowing Wycliffe's teaching on transubstantiation to go unchecked for so long. After his death they bitterly remarked that he had failed to nip this heresy in the bud.

Everything was now in Courtenay's favour. John of Gaunt's policy of aggression against clerical wealth had been mildly supported at court. The Peasants' Revolt changed that. From now on Courtenay and the church could rely on the full support of Parliament. Until the age of the Tudors, there was to be an unwritten alliance between church and state. Courtenay could always count on the secular arm to help him crush heresy. While the revolt had changed the views of the nobility, the ensuing persecution was essentially religious. The heretics must be rooted out like weeds from the garden.

Courtenay, however, was Catholic to the core. Although he longed to commence the persecution, it was not until he received the pall[1] from Rome in May 1382 that he felt that his investment was complete and that he could commence trials and persecution with full papal authority. Until May he even refused to allow the cross to be borne before him, because, he felt, he was not yet truly an archbishop.

But on 17 May 1382, armed with this full papal power, Courtenay convened a synod at Blackfriars (the same building in which Henry VIII later appeared when he sought a divorce from Catherine of Aragon). Courtenay drew up a list of heresies and headed the list by Wycliffe's teaching on transubstantiation. This was followed by his teaching that a priest in mortal sin could not administer the sacraments and that our Lord did not ordain the ceremonies of the mass. Wycliffe's views on church government (which did not permit a pope) and his teachings on the uselessness of the regular orders were also declared heretical. The Lollards were placed under the ban of the church. War had been declared and no quarter would be given.

It is recorded that about 2 p.m. on 19 May, just as the synod were declaring the items on the list to be heretical, an earthquake shook the City of London, filling the hearts of the bishops and clergy alike with terror. The whole building shook and many present felt that this was God's judgement on them for condemning the Lollards.

Courtenay sternly ordered the frightened bishops and clergy to resume their seats. 'Know you not that the noxious vapours which catch fire in the bosom of the earth, and give rise to these phenomena which alarm you, lose all their force when they burst forth?' he asked. 'Well, in the like manner, by rejecting the wicked from our community, we shall put an end to the convulsions of the church.'

The clergy reluctantly took their seats and continued their work. But the earthquake appears to have been particularly violent for England, casting down pinnacles and steeples. Wycliffe was quick to take advantage of this in his preaching. As some Lollards said, 'If our master has been condemned by the bishops, then they have certainly been condemned by God.'

The prelates continued their work on the list of so-called heresies, adding a number which were later firmly denied by Wycliffe. One of these was the proposition that God ought to obey the devil! It is worthy of note that in all these discussions, and they must have been very heated ones, Wycliffe's name was not even mentioned — only his teachings. Nor was John summoned to appear before the synod, although his followers were.

Courtenay's next move was to deal firmly with the seat of the trouble — Oxford. During the winter of 1381 and early 1382 there had been considerable strife and tension at the university. Roughly speaking, Oxford was divided between those who cried out for John's scalp (the friars and regular orders) and those who supported him (the secular orders and students). The latter did so more because of Wycliffe's democratic form of teaching than because they truly believed his doctrines or wanted to read the Bible. The Peasants' Revolt had made them feel that they wanted more justice.

Oxford at this time had no bishop and came under the jurisdiction of the Bishop of Lincoln, but he was a convenient distance from Oxford. Without question, it was the leading university of Europe. Rome was so far away that the chancellor and professors could, if they wished, laugh at the pope and his bans.

Strong rivalry, and even hatred, existed between the secular priests, who formed the bulk of the faculty, and the monks and friars who had encroached into the university's territory and were constantly proselytizing students. The secular priests (Wycliffe was a secular priest) looked on this with bitterness. They came under the bishop as well as the Chancellor of Oxford. The majority of monks and friars were only answerable to the pope, apart from their local abbot or prior.

Courtenay's synod had decided that each bishop must arrest any unlicensed preachers in his diocese and the Crown agreed to back this action. But in the case of Oxford, not only was it a hundred miles from the Bishop of Lincoln, but it enjoyed a strong independence that made it hostile to any interference — even from the Crown. To be fair, its learning and the leading scholars it had produced made it very proud.

Earlier in Wycliffe's life, when he had attacked church property, he had even had the support of the friars. Later, after he censured them and criticized their wealth and teachings, they became his strongest enemies. His attack on the Eucharistic doctrine was the last straw. They were now his bitter enemies and waited for their chance of revenge. But the secular clergy and students at Oxford, even when they did not agree with his new doctrine, still felt that they should support John, 'the flower of Oxford'.

John of Gaunt had rushed down to the university when Wycliffe's teaching on the mass was first made public and tried to get him to withdraw this 'new teaching'. Wycliffe refused and the alliance between the two came to an end. Gaunt was as orthodox as Henry VIII and referred to Wycliffe's teaching as that 'detestable opinion on the Sacrament of the altar'.

Shortly before the Peasants' Revolt, a new chancellor had been elected at Oxford, Robert Rygge. He looked more favourably upon John's writings than his predecessor had done. During his term of office, Wycliffism became popular at Oxford, largely because the students and faculty felt that Wycliffe was their champion and one whom they should defend. Although Rygge was not a Lollard, he nevertheless permitted John's doctrines to be preached in church and taught in lecture-hall.

Feeling between the parties mounted higher after the revolt. The seculars accused the friars of having stirred up the poor by religious influence and preaching. Nicholas Hereford, who had worked hard with Wycliffe on the first translation of the Bible, preached against the mendicant orders wherever he could, and carried with him the bulk of the university. The friars felt so much endangered that they appealed to John of Gaunt, but he refused to become involved.

Hereford preached before the faculty in St Mary's, Oxford in February 1382 and exhorted the authorities to exclude monks and friars from all degrees. They complained to Rygge, yet not only did he refuse to do anything but he listened with interest to his two proctors who had been at St Mary's and had applauded Hereford. Wycliffism appeared to have gained control in Oxford, supported by both 'town and gown'. In desperation a deputation of monks and friars made their way to London to complain to Courtenay.

The 'Council of the Earthquake' was famous for another reason. It was the time of reunion between the bishops and the mendicant orders, who had been at loggerheads for many years. When the deputation from Oxford appeared, it placed the seal on the new alliance. From now on they must work together or the heretics might win. They were like Herod and Pilate who 'that day . . . became friends' (Luke 23:12).

The bishops warmly welcomed this opportunity to win back the seat of learning. They sent a message to Rygge rebuking him for permitting Hereford to preach. He was ordered to support Stokes, an Oxford friar with a hot temper. This was like throwing oil on to a fire. Not only had Courtenay interfered with Oxford, but he had taken the friars' side. Overnight most of Oxford became ardent Wycliffites. No bishop had any power over them, they claimed, even in cases of heresy.

Soon uproar filled the town. Students joined with the town militia. Another alliance had taken place, that of 'town with gown'. Rygge came to church with the Mayor of Oxford, while students and citizens came with swords under their gowns. Stokes and the friars were overawed. Later, Stokes received open insults. The Blackfriars condemnation of Wycliffe's teaching was published by Rygge but treated as a mere joke. Rygge now publicly defied Courtenay.

Later, when Rygge had cooled down, he thought it expedient to go to London and explain matters lest he lose his post. On his arrival he was charged with supporting the Lollards. Rygge had indiscreetly applauded teaching against the mass, and in the eyes of the synod, this was a cardinal sin. His courage oozed away as he faced the hierarchy. He confessed that he had been wrong and fell on his knees to beg for pardon. It was granted only because William of Wykeham pleaded for him. Rygge was sent back to Oxford with stern orders to suspend Wycliffe, Hereford, Repingdon and other leaders. He told the synod that he felt that it would be difficult to enforce Courtenay's orders. 'Then the university is the favourer of heresy!' Courtenay thundered. Later the king summoned Rygge and ordered him to obey the synod's decrees.

But when Rygge reached Oxford his courage apparently returned. The orders that he brought infuriated the secular clergy and it looked as if Oxford would rise in revolt. However, on 13 July the king ordered Rygge to banish Wycliffe, Hereford, Repingdon and John Aston from the university and town within seven days. This time Rygge knew that he must obey.

The 'Council of the Earthquake' had not yet finished its

work. Rygge had been dealt with. The next on their list was John Aston, a leading Lollard preacher. Later Hereford and Repingdon were also summoned before them.

John Aston, who later became one of the greatest Lollard missionaries, enjoyed great popularity with the people. When he came before the Council of Blackfriars, the citizens of London burst into the hall during his trial. This gave Aston new courage. He refused to agree to the Catholic teaching on transubstantiation. Instead, he declared that the matter was beyond his understanding, though he wished to believe what the Scriptures and the church taught.

These words sound innocent, but they were understood well enough by his listeners. Wycliffe had argued that Scripture was on his side and that the church had taught as he did concerning the Eucharist for more than 1,000 years. Fearing that the laymen listening would understand, Courtenay ordered Aston to speak in Latin, but he continued to speak louder than ever in English. Aston was appealing, not to the bishops, but to the people of London. For this he was condemned, but the synod did not dare to harm him.

A few days later a broadsheet appeared, in English and Latin. In this Aston explained his views on the mass. It was circulated throughout the city and posted up in the streets. The citizens of London showed a real interest in the controversy. As one historian has pointed out, the medieval church and her enemies must have been aware that the 'miracle' of the mass had a close connection with the power of the clergy over the people.

When Hereford and Repingdon appeared at Blackfriars, the same key question was put to them. What did they believe the mass to be? They repudiated most of Wycliffe's condemned theses but reserved their opinion on the mass and the mendicancy of the friars. It is doubtful if they were ever heart and soul with Wycliffe, but at least they gave him the benefit of university opinion on his teaching on the Eucharist. For this Courtenay condemned and excommunicated them on 1 July.

After the king's orders to Rygge, these men knew that they could not return to Oxford. Aston and Repingdon went into hiding for some time, while Hereford, convinced that he had discovered the truth, set off for Rome to appeal to the pope. Others have had the same conviction. They have believed, as did Hereford, that the pope would surely change his teachings if the truth were once shown to him. Hereford's only reward was to be cast into the Castle of St Angelo for two years.

Wycliffe, who had taken hardly any part in this controversy, was probably at Lutterworth using his pen while it all took place. The king's mandate had closed to him the town where he had studied, taught and lectured. Apart from this, John suffered a stroke some time in 1382. Many details of his life at this point are not clearly recorded. But neither the mandate nor the stroke prevented him from using his pen. He felt a call to this field of service and, much as he regretted being banned from Oxford, he pressed on with the work in feverish haste.

Doubtless, Wycliffe feared that he might suffer another stroke. He thought of his followers more as missionaries and considered what was the best way to train and prepare them for their work. Scholarship now counted for little. 'If divinity were learned on that manner that apostles did,' Wycliffe wrote, 'it should profit much more than it doth now by state of school, as priests now without such state [i.e. scholarship] profit much more than men of such state . . . And thus men of school travail vainly for to get new subtleties . . . and the profit of Holy Church by this way is put back.' Wycliffe was both disappointed and disgusted by the reception that his teaching on the mass received in the colleges. 'An unlearned man with God's grace does more for the church than many graduates,' he wrote. John began to regard scholastic studies as a breeding ground for heresies.

This change of attitude was both good and bad for John and his work. It was good because it fitted him for his work as a popular reformer. It enabled him to get on to the wavelength of the average Englishman. He had turned from the Latin-reading students to the English-speaking people. But it was bad because it had its weaknesses. Many of the 'poor priests' that he trained were too simple and ignorant. This was because Wycliffe had connected his reform with the idea of apostolic poverty. He took Christ's words, 'Sell your possessions and give to the poor' (Matthew 19:21) as being of universal application and for all time. He failed to appreciate that God did not ask every rich person to do the same (for example, Abraham in the Old Testament or Joseph of Arimathea in the New Testament).

Wycliffe had fallen into the same trap as Francis of Assisi. This resulted in the wealthy being almost banned from becoming Lollards, yet they were certainly the best educated. Not many rich young men could be found who would 'sell what they possessed'. More and more Lollards were drawn from the lower and uneducated classes. After all, they had little to lose if they renounced their possessions. This lack of balance in his followers constituted a grave weakness.

When the bishops appealed to the king for help against the Lollards in May 1382, Richard had responded quickly, if illegally. Courtenay knew from bitter experience that unless backed by the state, the church persecuted the heretic in vain. A brief parliament sat from 7 May to 22 May. After the departure (or at least in the absence) of the Commons, the king and the lords drew up an ordinance to imprison any who maintained or taught Wycliffe's doctrines. Constitutionally, this was illegal since the Commons had not been consulted. It never became statutory law but it gave Courtenay the encouragement that he needed. In July the king sent a writ to every bishop, ordering him to arrest all Lollards. There must be no heresy in England. Despite all this, Wycliffe was left untouched, but the fact that he had suffered a stroke may partly account for this. Also, Wycliffe had now retired from Oxford to Lutterworth, after being silenced as a professor. In addition, Courtenay did not like to have John of Gaunt as an antagonist. He had not forgotten the scene in St Paul's. While Gaunt was reputed to have abandoned Wycliffe, he was a man of devious ways: no one could be absolutely certain of him.

Although Wycliffe's inner circle of supporters, such as Aston, Repingdon and Hereford, gradually shrank, and his physical strength grew less, yet his moral strength increased. Martyrdom has never been attractive and the more intelligent of Wycliffe's followers could see the storm-clouds ahead. They decided that it would be prudent to leave him until the prospects brightened.

Parliament was summoned again in October 1382 and met in November. The Commons insisted that the king's ordinance, drawn up in their absence, should be annulled. 'Forasmuch as that statute was made without our consent, and never authorized by us; and as it never was our meaning to bind ourselves, or our successors, to the prelates, any more than our ancestors have done before us, we pray that the aforesaid statute may be repealed.'

If the king and the barons were keen to suppress heresy, the knights of the shires were more concerned with preserving the Englishman's freedom from interference by the clergy. They had not forgotten the Magna Carta and England was not accustomed to religious persecution. The Inquisition had been founded and at work in Europe for over a century but the heretic at the stake was almost unknown in England at that time. The church was growing unpopular; if she sought to take action such as was common in Europe, she would become even more unpopular. She certainly could not count on the backing of the Commons. They had no desire to be priest-ridden.

But Oxford was not in such a strong position. In November 1382, Courtenay summoned a convocation to meet in Oxford 'for the suppression of heresy'. The 'purification' of Oxford was at hand. Wycliffe remained at Lutterworth but his former close followers could not escape. Chancellor Rygge was now an obedient servant of the convocation. Philip Repingdon, unwilling to sacrifice his career, had recanted in October and been re-established in his former post. He again publicly confessed his former heresies before the Oxford Convocation. He later rose to be bishop and, finally, cardinal. During the reign of Henry IV, Repingdon persecuted the Lollards.

John Aston also appeared before the convocation. Two months previously (after his trial at Blackfriars) he had preached Wycliffe's doctrines in Gloucester and travelled through England, staff in hand, preaching with zeal. But when he faced the bishops at Oxford, Aston pleaded ignorance on the question of the Eucharist. He was ordered to discuss it with Rygge and other doctors. Later, he professed to be convinced and read his recantation before the bishops, denying that the host was 'merely bread' and apologizing

Persecution

for his rudeness at Blackfriars. He, too, was restored to his former post.

The secular priests and students looked on helplessly. Courtenay's victory appeared to be complete. If Lollardy raised its head again at Oxford it would promptly be crushed. Over a hundred and twenty years later the popular Reformer, Hugh Latimer, was sent to Cambridge by his father because Oxford was still remembered by some as the one-time heretical university.[2] Even free discussion had become impossible. This action by king and bishops finally shut the doors of Oxford to Wycliffe. He was banished to Lutterworth for life.[3]

1. Woollen vestment worn by pope or archbishop.
2. For more detail see Latimer's biography, *Such a Candle,* published by Evangelical Press.
3. Some Victorian writers (and others) have stated that Wycliffe appeared before both the Council of Blackfriars and the Convocation of Oxford. But as Professor G. M. Trevelyan points out, there is no record of this in Courtenay's *Lambeth Register* (which records the business of both the council and the convocation). The appearance of Wycliffe would have been a highlight for the register. Why then was he not mentioned? The most obvious answer is that these writers based their statements on the writings of Knighton, a Leicester monk, who indulged in more than a little romancing and wishful thinking. He even claims that Wycliffe recanted before the Council of Blackfriars.

13.
The gospel spreads

1382–1384

The closure of Oxford to Wycliffe had one good effect. Several Oxford men decided that if the colleges no longer permitted free discussion then Lutterworth must be their centre. They gathered round Wycliffe and this strengthened the Lollard cause. The brains from Oxford acted as leaven among the simpler folk who made up the majority of his 'poor preachers'.

Another encouraging factor for Wycliffe was the insistence by Parliament in October 1382 that the illegal ordinance drawn up in May be withdrawn. When this news reached the ears of the Lollards, it was like a shot in the arm to men who felt uncertain about their future. The Commons' demand certainly gave the Lollards time to grow and spread throughout England and as they did so, their teaching became planted in the hearts of many people.

This was God's timing: a century earlier there would have been no difficulty in getting both houses, Lords and Commons, to agree to support the bishops in their plans for the persecution of heretics. Now they were less reverent to the church and all it stood for. It is impossible to say how many members were actually heretical or pro-Wycliffe. Merchants and the upper classes had certainly been reached by John's teaching, especially the country gentry. William Langland, the fourteenth-century poet and the author of *Piers Plowman,* states that even before Wycliffe and his teachings became widely known, the gentry often discussed religion just 'as if they were clergy':

> At meat in their mirths, when minstrels are still,
> Then tell they of the Trinity a tale or two,

The gospel spreads

> And bring forth a bald reason and quote St Bernard,
> And put forth a presumption to prove the sooth.
> Thus they drivel at their dais the deity to know,
> And gnaw God with the gorge when their gut is full.

Langland's language and description seem crude to us, verging on blasphemy. But this is fourteenth-century language. To people who believed that they actually 'ate' God (i.e. Christ) when they consumed the consecrated wafer in the mass, it would appear quite reasonable and at least as reverent as the language used by the majority of priests. One thing it does reveal: their tendency to free thought and a desire to be independent of the priests. But this refers to the upper and middle classes. The same dislike of the clergy and irreverence for the church also existed among many of the peasants and yeomen, as they showed in the Peasants' Revolt, when they were prepared to sack monasteries and kill archbishops.

But not all were like this. One man who had made a name for himself in the revolt was Bishop Spencer of Norwich. He has been aptly named 'the fighting bishop'. Spencer was more a soldier than a bishop and the peasants who revolted in East Anglia were dealt with ruthlessly and mercilessly. In 1382 Pope Urban of Rome sent a commission to Spencer to raise an English army and conduct a crusade against his rival's supporters, the French Clementists (supporters of Pope Clement of Avignon).

Spencer speedily responded to Urban's call and began recruiting immediately. The friars, those devout servants of the pope, used all their guile and talent to persuade men to join and women to support the crusade, largely in East Anglia but to a lesser extent elsewhere. England nodded with approval; she had been at war with France, off and on, for many years. Urban's quarrel was, in some ways, her quarrel too. Money flowed in from the faithful. Men and women gave their gold, silver and jewellery, in the belief that they were securing for themselves and their friends absolution from their sins. Many men joined as soldiers or archers (at their own expense, of course. No pay could be expected since it was a crusade for God and for the church.) Absolution was denied to any who refused to give in proportion to their income. Spencer distributed indulgences under papal licence to those who gave generously, which absolved both the living and the dead from their sins. One is reminded of Tetzel, the Dominican indulgence seller who roused Luther to write the ninety-five theses. Spencer's crusade shows clearly how many people were still blind supporters of the church.

The soldiers embarked for France in 1383, but the crusade was a dismal failure. A man capable of leading a small troop of soldiers against many hundreds of ill-armed peasants proved to be totally incapable of leading a large army. Spencer was defeated, driven back and had to retreat with a mere handful of men.

On his return to England, Spencer was impeached by the Commons for misconduct in the war, found guilty by the Lords and, as punishment, forfeited his episcopal temporalities. It was unfortunate that he did not lose his episcopate entirely because Spencer had sworn that he would burn any Lollard who set foot in his diocese. It is interesting to note that later, after he had disappeared from the scene, Norfolk and Suffolk became the hotbed of the Lollards.

But Spencer's crusade roused Wycliffe to use his pen more vigorously than ever. When people flocked to support the crusade he must have felt that all his work had been in vain. Surely, if ever he had a right to be bitter, it was now. Here were two men, both of whom claimed to be the spiritual 'father' of all Christendom, yet each was goading and urging his spiritual children to fight the other. In fact it would have appeared to people of that day that the climax could eventually result in Armageddon.

Yet despite the apparent support in the Commons, Wycliffe's voice was the only one heard in protest. As he knew the important part played by the mendicant friars in recruiting and gathering money for the crusade, he wrote another tract called *Objections to the Friars*. In this he summed up all his previous censures against them, their practices and teachings. He accused them of upholding 'CAIM'S castles for Satan'. 'CAIM' was a word created by Wycliffe, using the initial letters of the four mendicant orders: 'C' for Carmelites, 'A' for Augustinians, 'I' for Jacobites or Dominicans and 'M' for Minorites or Franciscans. In this tract he refers to the sacramental controversy over the mass, the papal schism and Spencer's war in Flanders.

The gospel spreads

The object of the war or crusade, claimed Wycliffe, was 'to make Christ's vicar the wealthiest (man) in the world'.

In another tract — and he wrote many at this time — he asks the question, 'Are wars lawful?' His answer to this briefly is that, without a special injunction from God (who is the Lord of battles also) they are just as indefensible under the Christian dispensation as they were in the Jewish theocracy (i.e., in Old Testament times). Even wars of self-defence are not given much support in his writing. He does not, however, tell his readers how the quarrels between nations should be settled. He was a man ahead of his time and if he proposed pacifist teaching, he must have known that it would be a waste of time to put this forth. It would only have brought him scorn and derision.

Another tract, called the *Trialogue*, put forth comprehensively and systematically all his major truths and arguments. The *Trialogue* was printed years later, in 1525, since it was as important for the Reformation as when it first appeared in 1384. But few realized its value when it first appeared. In this work, three characters take the stage, *Aletheia* (truth), *Phronesis* (understanding) and *Pseudes* (falsehood). These three persons argue between them, and in the conversation or trialogue, Wycliffe brings forth great truths. The difference between the pope and Christ, and the canons of Romanism and the Bible, stand out clearly. This tract was undoubtedly one of his greatest works.

The young king, Richard II, was married in January 1382 to Princess Anne, sister of King Wenceslaus of Bohemia (of carol fame). It is not surprising to find that this was a purely diplomatic move, connected with both the English enmity with France and the rival popes. England was a loyal supporter of the pope at Rome and Wenceslaus had considered wedding his sister to the son of the King of France, who supported the Avignon pope. Pope Urban of Rome urged Wenceslaus to have his sister married to Richard instead. Since Bohemian kings were notoriously poor and Wenceslaus was no exception, he gladly accepted the pope's advice and the large sum of money offered by Westminster. The diplomatic move proved unsuccessful but it affected England and spread Wycliffe's teaching to the far side of Europe.

It is ironic that the pope should have urged that the

marriage take place. He failed to realize that this would help to spread Wycliffe's teaching overseas. Before and after the wedding there was a constant flow of Bohemians between Prague and London and vice versa. In this way Wycliffe's theological works were read by many of them in Latin, the international language, and also taken back to Prague, since there were a number of scholars who passed from Prague to Oxford and returned home with Wycliffe's ideas and books. In this interchange of scholars, some grasped Wycliffe's teaching and realized that this was what they had been searching for.

This marriage was to bring about another schism, far worse to Rome than that of Avignon. The University of Prague and the towns and villages of Bohemia were ripe for the seed which brought forth a speedy harvest. Wycliffe's works precipitated reform in Bohemia when they reached the hands of John Hus. When Jerome of Prague, a friend of Hus, returned from Oxford in 1402 with more of Wycliffe's works, especially his *Dialogue* and *Trialogue*, Hus read them avidly. These writings helped to water the seed sown. Soon Rome faced a bigger problem in Bohemia than she had done in England. All Wycliffe's books were ordered to be surrendered and burnt. Then persecution began.

A Bohemian psalter of 1572 shows, in a picture, Wycliffe striking the spark, Hus kindling the coals while Luther brandishes the lighted torch of truth.[1] This is an apt illustration and one that would doubtless have gladdened Wycliffe's heart.

Sad to say, that heart was not destined to beat much longer. John Purvey, one of the Lollard preachers, stayed with Wycliffe at the rectory and constantly attended his master. Wycliffe no longer travelled around; all his work was done in the study at Lutterworth or in the pulpit of the church. His pen and brain remained active to the end.

What end did he expect? To be taken captive to Rome and thrown into a dungeon on one of the seven hills, or a martyr's end at Oxford or London? We do not know. But we can be sure that the 'poor preachers' who returned to Lutterworth were still encouraged by John and sent forth again to bring the good news of the gospel to the people of England.

The gospel spreads

Wycliffe appears to have suffered from a form of paralysis after the stroke when he retired to Lutterworth, which limited him in his activities. But at the end of December 1384 he was suddenly struck with extreme paralysis and had to be carried to his bedroom. There he lay for forty-eight hours until, on 31 December 1384, the man who gave England her first Bible passed away.

He was laid to rest in Lutterworth churchyard but even his mortal remains were not permitted to 'rest in peace'. In 1413 a synod in Rome condemned John's writings as heretical and two years later, on 4 May 1415, the Council of Constance (which was about to try Hus and Jerome) formally condemned Wycliffe (and his works) as 'the leader of heresy in that age'. It then ordered that his body be exhumed and burned. All his writings were ordered to be burned also, 'lest they lead the faithful astray'.

Soon after this Wycliffe's body was dug up, burned and the ashes thrown into the River Swift. The Swift flows into the River Wye, which joins the River Severn, which in turn empties itself into the ocean. As one old historian (Fuller) remarks, this illustrates how Wycliffe's doctrines were to be carried to the furthest corners of the earth.

> Of the book that had been a sealed up book,
>   He tore the clasps, that the nation,
> With eyes unbandaged might thereon look,
>   And learn to read salvation.
>
> A light was struck — a light which showed
>   How hideous were Error's features,
> And how perverted the law, bestowed
>   By heaven to guide its creatures.
>
> At first for that spark, amidst the dark,
>   The friar his fear dissembled;
> But soon at the fame of Wycliffe's name,
>   The throne of St Peter trembled.
>
>   Moir.

---

1. H. B. Workman, *John Wyclif*, Vol. I, p. 8 (Oxford 1926).

14.
Wycliffe's teaching

'On the Feast of the Passion of St Thomas, Archbishop of Canterbury — that organ of the devil — that enemy of the church — that author of confusion to the common people — that idol of heretics — that image of hypocrites — that restorer of schism — that storehouse of lies — that sink of flattery — John Wycliffe, being struck by the horrible judgement of God . . . until Saint Sylvester's Day, on which he breathed out his malicious spirit into the abodes of darkness.'

Such a bitter and vicious account of Wycliffe's death by Walsingham, if he is anything to judge by, shows what rejoicing there must have been among John's enemies. But, quite apart from the facts that have emerged in this study of his life, such jubilation by those who were his enemies proves that Wycliffe was not just an eccentric professor who was forced to resign from Oxford and live in obscurity. Men or women who rouse others to such a fanatical pitch as Walsingham's prove that they have 'trodden' on the spiritual, intellectual or political 'toes' of others.

At this point let us look back and see what Wycliffe did achieve. How far did he go? What doctrines or practices did he correct on biblical principles?

Neither his friends nor his enemies could or did deny the practical side; they had the Lollards with them and they were seen and heard by many throughout England. The Bible that he and his colleagues translated was used by these men. These two facts are written in the pages of history. We will ignore the religio/political matters that he dealt with.

But what were his achievements on the theological side? Before looking briefly at these, it would be as well to recognize that, unlike Luther and the other Reformers, Wycliffe

Wycliffe's teaching

appears to have been a solitary person. All his rediscoveries of scriptural truth were obtained by a study of the Bible and the writings of old theologians (mainly the church fathers) when he was on his own. The friends who gathered round him came later. But they came rather as disciples to one who had become a famous teacher and who had unearthed some great treasures.

The key doctrine for all Bible-loving Christians must surely be the one for which Luther became famous, justification by faith. It was spelt out so clearly in the sixteenth century that any who did not follow the example of these Reformers were regarded as 'unsound' in doctrine. It would not be unkind to say that, for some, 'justification by faith' became a catch-phrase. Since Wycliffe did not use it as did the later Reformers, even Philip Melanchthon, Luther's colleague, stigmatized Wycliffe's theology as being tainted with Pelagianism (this doctrine teaches that man has a natural ability to do good, that he is born innocent, the primacy of the human will in salvation, and the possibility of sinless perfection).

When one reads Wycliffe's biblical teaching on the sovereignty of God, on election and predestination, Melanchthon's accusation seems laughable and ridiculous. That man, who is utterly dependent on God's grace, mercy and love could, like a petulant child, turn from evil to good, when and if he wishes, or ignore the salvation offered by Christ, is nonsensical. As Professor Lechler states, in Wycliffe's teaching 'every . . . Christian owes all that he possesses in his inner life to the regeneration which is the fruit of election'.

Wycliffe stated clearly that the merit of Christ is sufficient to redeem mankind from hell; that faith in him is sufficient for salvation; that those who truly follow him are justified by his justice and made righteous by participation in his righteousness. But to be fair to Melanchthon, Wycliffe did not propound his teachings in the systematic way that the sixteenth-century Reformers wanted. He wrote so much and so widely that his teachings on the fundamental Christian doctrines were often mixed up with other secondary matters.

As we have seen from Lechler's statement, the doctrine of election was clearly taught by Wycliffe, but his teaching on predestination was closely linked with that on good works. In other words, action, not dogma, was the test for the man who claimed to be a Christian. In this respect Wycliffe's teaching was very much like that of Luther. One laid an emphasis on works to prove that a man had faith, while the other stressed the need for a living faith which would of necessity result in good works. We can be quite sure that Wycliffe would not have called the letter of James 'an epistle of straw', as did Luther.

But there is one point on which Wycliffe differed greatly from the later Reformers: that is, on his teaching on purgatory. He retained his belief in this to the end of his days. But, to judge from his later writings, his mind remained in a state of indecision. One thing to note is that he taught clearly that the prayers of the pious layman were of more value to those in purgatory than the prayers of a useless prelate. He also divided the church into three groups: the militant (the church on earth), the reposing or resting (those in purgatory) and the triumphant (those in heaven). Wycliffe spoke of the sabbath as prefiguring the rest of those who sleep in purgatory. Clearly, he pictured purgatory as a different state from that which the Roman teaching describes. Their dogma regards it as a state of temporal punishment where the 'fires of purgatory' can purify the soul from venial sins.

We need to remind ourselves that Wycliffe was born into an extremely superstitious world and the church had imbibed much of this. How, by the grace of God, John was enabled to see and teach so much of God's truths in that dark age is truly amazing.

Closely allied to purgatory are auricular confession of one's sins to a priest and papal indulgences. There was no uncertainty in Wycliffe's voice or pen when he denounced and attacked these, and we cannot but admire his courage when we remember that both of these provided Rome with a very large income. Any person who attacked Rome's major source of revenue asked for trouble, yet Wycliffe did so unhesitatingly. He proclaimed to the country in plain, homely English that pardons and indulgences were mere forgeries. He denied that either penance or confession was necessary for the true Christian. Confession, to a suitable person, Wycliffe said, could be good and useful, if it was

Wycliffe's teaching

voluntary. But compulsory confession to a priest was bad and therefore not truly a sacrament, as Rome claims it to be. He quite rightly declared that it had been introduced into the church after the apostolic era in more corrupt days.

Wycliffe had no use for saints and their canonization by Rome, or pilgrimages to their shrines. The use of images, considered by Rome to be 'the *books* of unlettered laymen', he reluctantly conceded, but compared them to the wedding ring worn by a wife as a symbol of her love and faithfulness to her husband. While he considered their use lawful, he did not regard them as safe and kept a constant eye on their misuse. Wycliffe saw that idolatry lurked just round the corner in this practice and he thought it would be better if all images of so-called 'saints' were removed and destroyed.

It was when Wycliffe dealt with the papacy, papal interdicts and excommunication that we see his sternest and harshest judgements pronounced. That a mortal man, born in sin, could elevate himself to such a position and use the title 'pontiff', as used by the pagan Roman emperors, really angered Wycliffe. It could be said that his life was one continual protest against the authority of the pope, temporal and spiritual. No bishop or pope could possess spiritual infallibility or secular supremacy, Wycliffe declared. So all his days were spent in incessant warfare against this 'master of the emperor, this fellow of God, this Deity on earth' and his army of clerical satellites. 'No', Wycliffe declared, 'he is not the "Vicar of Christ", his title should be "Antichrist"'. The 'power of the keys', seen chiefly in excommunication, was regarded, not only by the Roman church, but by the Eastern church (Greek Orthodox), as the axis on which the ecclesiastical system revolved and without which no Christian community deserved the name of 'church'.

Yet despite this, John was prepared to write and speak against the pope and then propound what he believed Scripture taught concerning the church. It consists, Wycliffe said, of the church visible and the church invisible. The former is a mixture of those ordained to bliss and hypocrites doomed to perdition; but the latter (the invisible or spiritual) is the vital thing for man, since it consists only of Christ's elect, his saints, those for whom he shed his blood. All are equal since all are saved by grace. Prince and peasant alike humbly worship the Lord and confess that only by his love and grace have they been saved. The visible church should be governed in the same way as the primitive church. This had only two officers, the deacon and the presbyter or bishop. Popes, cardinals, archbishops and similar additions were man's invention and should be swept away. The church should return to the form of government revealed in Scripture.

But, of course, Wycliffe's most explosive teaching was that on the Lord's Supper or Eucharist. As we noted earlier, this was and is the centre of the Roman faith, since her priestly power revolves round it. When Wycliffe attacked this teaching, it was like a nuclear explosion in theological circles.

Now all philosophical and theological disguise was swept away. He was clearly a heretic in Rome's eyes. No one dared to deny transubstantiation or the power of the priest to change the elements into the literal, physical body and blood of Christ. This was where the priestly power of Rome centred. To take this away was like removing the keystone from an archway: remove it and the archway collapses. But Wycliffe went forward boldly and showed that the keystone could and should be removed. To do this demanded immense courage, since he knew that death could be the penalty for such audacious heretics. It is true that Wycliffe did not go as far as the majority of the later Reformers and appears to have held the doctrine of consubstantiation. But then so did Luther; this was where he parted company with Calvin, Zwingli and other Reformers. This should not therefore surprise us in a man living nearly a hundred and fifty years earlier.

But the most vital thing for the people of Wycliffe's day, as it should be for us, was his translation of the Bible and the place that he gave to Scripture. It was on this that all his teaching was based. He first restored the Bible to its rightful place as God's written Word to man. He contended for the supreme authority and entire sufficiency of Scripture. Wycliffe would have agreed whole-heartedly with Dr Benjamin B. Warfield when he stated, 'The Spirit's superintendence extends to the choice of the words by the human

Wycliffe's teaching

authors (verbal inspiration) . . . thus securing, among other things, that entire truthfulness which is everywhere presupposed in and asserted for Scripture by the biblical writers (inerrancy).' The Bible was God's Word to man, claimed Wycliffe, and had been preserved for him through the ages, while decisions of popes and councils were as nothing. The all-important question was 'What does the Bible say?' The traditions of the church were likewise brushed aside; had not the Pharisees used tradition rather than Scripture? The church was merely repeating their sin.

Especially important for the ordinary man or woman was his insistence on the right of every Christian to study and know the Bible for himself. It was not just to be the ultimate authority in all doctrinal arguments, but the daily guidebook for the Christian. The problems introduced by the Scholastic theologians were swept away by John. Scripture was *not* to be interpreted allegorically but literally (apart from poetic passages). In this way Wycliffe removed the barrier to understanding the Bible.

From this it was almost inevitable that Wycliffe would provide an English translation. As he had found in his own experience that the only true guide for man was God's Word, and believed that all should read it (not just the priest), he planned an English translation. But again he had to defy the hierarchy since the Council of Valencia had officially forbidden laymen to read the Bible.

The problems of translating Scripture have been mentioned but to a man of Wycliffe's calibre and talent they were no deterrent. He went forward boldly and, aided by friends, gave England its first Bible in the vernacular. This inspired and helped Tyndale in the sixteenth century. Wycliffe's ministry, as he laboured to translate the Bible, has given the English-speaking world its greatest heritage and set an example for others to follow.

15.
Early history of the Lollards (1382—1401)

1382–1401

When in November 1382 the House of Commons insisted that the illegal ordinance introduced by Courtenay and the Lords be annulled, the Lollard preachers then had a relatively free hand for several years. Sometimes a bishop, sometimes the king, began to hunt a certain preacher who had made himself too troublesome. Frequently, however, the 'poor priest' defied the authorities and escaped. He used his wits and the common people gladly helped him. Even the local authorities were reluctant to help the church catch an innocent man. Generally speaking, public opinion strongly favoured the Lollards.

In the early days the Lollards flourished in three areas: the neighbourhood round Leicester, the West of England and the environs of London. From these centres the preachers went forth to spread Wycliffe's teaching. Like the ripples that come when a stone is dropped into a pond, so the Lollards spread out like waves from these centres. Later, new centres became established as the teaching became accepted and converts made. Space forbids our taking more than a brief glance at all their achievements. We can look at only a few in detail.

A glance at a map of England shows why Leicester became a centre. It lies twelve miles from Lutterworth. In Wycliffe's day it was the nearest town and it gave the Lollards a large congregation if they appeared on market day.

The 'poor preachers' recognized a ministry independent of Rome; their authority depended on the Word of God alone. They attacked the wealth of the clergy and the degenerate asceticism of the mendicant orders. Both were

Early history of the Lollards 119

wrong according to Scripture. They urged true Christian poverty together with a spiritually free life. The townsfolk gathered round the Lollards; frequently the 'poor preacher' had soldiers in his congregation. With armed men on the side of the Lollards, their enemies were even more reluctant to take action against them. It is said that even some of the nobility not only listened to their words, but acted on them and took down the images from their ancestral chapels.

It will give us some idea of the areas covered by these preachers up to the end of the fourteenth century if we realize that they affected the counties of Leicester, Northampton, Warwick, Worcester, Hereford, Gloucester, part of Monmouth, Berkshire, Wiltshire, Sussex, an area around London, and a small area around Canterbury. Astounding as it may appear to us, one writer claims that there is clear evidence of missionary effort by an English Lollard in the Adriatic as early as 1383.[1] So it should not surprise us to find that, after the turn of the century, the Lollards had reached parts of Scotland, especially the Cunningham district, Ayr and Kirkcudbrightshire.

It is thought that Scottish students at Oxford brought Wycliffe's teaching to their homeland and so prepared the way for Lollard preachers. In 1407 William Thorpe, who claimed to have followed Wycliffe for many years, when examined by Archbishop Arundel, admitted that he had preached in the north of England for twenty years. From the vagueness of his confession, this could easily have included parts of Scotland. But the first concrete proof of Lollardy in Scotland was in 1407 when James Reseby, an English priest who had escaped to Scotland, was condemned and burned at Perth. Three years later Quintin Folkhard, another Lollard, followed him and died in the same way. Evidence exists that, at the Council of Constance (which condemned Wycliffe and Hus), the Chancellor of Paris University complained of the spread of Lollardy in Scotland as well as in England.

This does not mean that the Lollards never reached the other counties of England. While it cannot be proved that they were widespread in Bedfordshire, Rutland, Hertfordshire, Salop, Derbyshire, Devonshire, Southampton or Dorset, a document in the Public Record Office shows that after the Oldcastle Rising (January 1414), commissioners were appointed to arrest any rebels found hiding in these counties. This makes it probable that the Lollards were active there. Another document is available that does prove that Lollards were to be found in other counties since it names Lollards and the pardons granted to them after this rising. These counties were Yorkshire, Bedfordshire, Chester, Derbyshire and Oxfordshire.

It should be noted that, in the early days, the Lollards went forward not just with faith in the Word of God, but also with confidence that official reforms would take place. Many felt that Parliament would eventually be persuaded to support them.

Wycliffe's condemnation at Oxford in 1382 was the first set-back to the Lollards, while his death two years later certainly did not encourage them. But some continued to hope that official recognition and support would be forthcoming. A number of Lollards followed Wycliffe's example and a steady stream of tracts in English poured forth from their pens. Some were new pamphlets, others were translations of Wycliffe's works in Latin. To crown it all, in 1395 John Purvey completed the second translation of the Bible. This was much more idiomatic than the previous translation and the ordinary people received it even more readily.

The first Lollard to make a considerable impression in the area near to Lutterworth, namely Leicester, was a priest called William Swynderby. He had moved away from the mainstream of the church because he had rebuked the 'merry wives of Leicester' for their frivolity and then become a hermit. Later he joined the Lollards.

The latter made their home in a small deserted chapel outside Leicester. They encouraged one another and debated and discussed the new doctrines. At this stage some of them were rather uncertain of Wycliffe's teaching on certain points. The debates cleared away this uncertainty. Swynderby preached in all the churches for miles around (mainly because, as a priest, he had access to the pulpits) and was well known in Loughborough, Melton Mowbray and Harborough. He was even able to preach in the big churches of Leicester until the Bishop of Lincoln forbad him to preach on sacred ground. From that time on Swynderby preached from a mill.

The crowds who gathered to hear him grew daily larger. Swynderby denounced the clergy, using Wycliffe's arguments against wealth and exhorting poverty. He urged people to withhold their tithes from evil clergy and warned husbands and fathers to beware of the priest and his intimacy with their wives and daughters. But he did not preach any kind of communism or suggest anything subversive to law and order.

Just as Swynderby was about to become the popular hero, Courtenay, who was in Oxford dealing with the heretics there, had him arrested and brought before the Bishop of Lincoln. As might be expected, the friars, who felt their influence on the people declining, drew up a list of Swynderby's heresies for the bishop. In true monkish fashion, they grossly exaggerated what he had said and done. The Mayor of Leicester and some of the leading citizens endeavoured to correct this by sending a document affirming that many of the friars' accusations were untrue. This was ignored and Swynderby was condemned to the stake.

According to some records, faggots to burn him were actually being collected when John of Gaunt passed through the town. It was only through Gaunt's intercession that Swynderby's life was spared. He had to recant all his imputed heresies in order to save his life.

This recantation caused Swynderby to lose favour in the eyes of the people of Leicester. He found it necessary to leave the town and neighbourhood. He went to Coventry and preached there for about a year, gaining many converts. Eventually the clergy of Coventry forced him to move and and he continued his work further into the West Country.

Leicester was not left without witness. Swynderby's friends and fresh helpers from Oxford continued the work. John Aston paid a flying visit to the town and preached against transubstantiation. He emphatically declared that in the mass the elements remained bread and wine. Swynderby had not dared to do this; he had made veiled references to the nature of the host but nothing more. But under Aston's preaching this doctrine became accepted among the Lollards of Leicester. Soon after this Aston, too, moved on.

After Wycliffe's death John Purvey, who was looked up to as a man specially well-versed in Wycliffe's teaching — since he was with the reformer until his death — moved on to the West of England. Now the Lollards in the little chapel near Leicester had to stand on their own feet. Prior to this, Purvey had often assisted them.

Basically, these men were popular preachers and lacked the scholarly approach of Wycliffe. They appealed more to common sense than did John. He had deprecated the worship of images but had been guarded in his teaching concerning these. The Leicester Lollards were, however, thorough iconoclasts and denounced the cult of image worship. In 1382 they found themselves short of firewood and so they pulled down a figure of St Catherine that stood in the deserted sanctuary and used it for fuel.

This created a sensation in Leicester. But it also showed a marked change in their outlook. From now on the Lollards became more outspoken against all forms of superstition. A contemporary chronicler records with horror how these heretics described all images as 'idols' and how St Mary of Lincoln was called by them 'the witch of Lincoln'.

As time went on, the chief matters for dispute between the Lollards and the orthodox were the nature of the Eucharist and the value of saints, images and shrines. It was now easy to recognize the 'poor priests' in their long russet-coloured gowns. They could easily be picked out in the crowd in the market-place. They had formed the habit of basing all their arguments on some teaching in 'God's Law', as did Wycliffe. The Lollards never preached any doctrines that were subversive and they often made good friends of the wealthy citizens and of the knights and gentry. In Leicestershire and Northamptonshire, Sir Thomas Latimer, a powerful local knight, welcomed them to any of his many manor-houses.

Friends like this enabled a 'poor priest' to spend a night in comfort at the moat-house after a long, tiring day on the road. He would be well fed with wine and venison, then on the next day he would be asked to preach to the people in the churchyard or even in the church. The knight stood by to prevent any interference from the hierarchy and when the parson felt that 'the better part of valour is discretion', he would leave the church door open to keep on good terms with the knight.

No one is certain when the first Lollard appeared in the West Country, but it is important to remember that Bristol and Gloucestershire were at that time part of the diocese of Worcester. The first Lollard missionary known to appear in those parts was John Aston who, staff in hand, walked into Gloucester in September 1382. He appears to have laboured there for five years.

After Wycliffe's death Purvey left Lutterworth and appeared in Bristol. True to form, he preached against the celebration of the mass. It was a mere human tradition, Purvey declared, and was neither biblical nor based on Christ's commands.

Nicholas Hereford landed in England in 1386, a sadder and wiser man. His efforts to convert the pope had been in vain and had resulted only in his imprisonment. He began to preach the Lollard doctrines near Canterbury and narrowly escaped capture by Courtenay. In 1387 Richard II was asked to help catch him and Hereford moved west to join Purvey and Aston. Six months later the Bishop of Worcester issued a mandate against all Lollard preachers in his diocese. He complained that Aston, Purvey and Hereford were moving around his diocese 'under a great cloak of secrecy'. They preached in public and also secretly in halls, chambers, parks and gardens. Even churches and churchyards were put at their service. Later Hereford not only returned to the bosom of 'mother church' but also assisted in the persecution of the Lollards.

There is one important difference between these men and those of later years — they were not ready to be martyrs. In October 1389 Courtenay visited the diocese of Lincoln and came to that hotbed of heresy, Leicester. For diplomatic reasons, he ignored Sir Thomas Latimer and other gentry. But a thorough heresy hunt began for the humbler Lollards. Of the nine names recorded only one was a priest; the others appear to have been tradesmen. Courtenay placed the town under an interdict until all the heretics were brought out of hiding. But surprising though it may seem, only four gave themselves up. The others remained in hiding.

In full pontifical splendour, Courtenay issued a 'sentence of excommunication with cross erected, candles lit and bells beating'. The four all recanted and were reconciled to the church. William Smith, who had burned the image of St Catherine for firewood, had to do penance with a crucifix in one hand and an image of the insulted saint in the other. Smith had taught himself to read and write and even studied theology. He had to surrender the books in which he had copied out parts of the New Testament and sayings of the church fathers. This was a great set-back for the Lollards of Leicester. Courtenay's action made them carry on their work with more secrecy and even tend to go underground to some extent.

It is commonly known that Richard II, far from favouring the Lollards, looked on them with great distaste and anger. Why, then, did he not commence a general persecution of the 'poor priests'? There is no simple answer to this, but certain factors should be noted which, taken together, could have tipped the scales in favour of the Lollards.

The first factor was Richard's fluctuating character. He could blow hot or cold without any apparent reason. During his life he showed alternately strength and weakness, clemency and vindictiveness. He appears to have been a very moody person. A man of this temperament is likely to have unexpected quarrels with his best friends.

After some high-handed actions by Richard in 1385, Archbishop Courtenay felt constrained to remonstrate with the king and warn him that he could drag England into civil war if he continued to act in this way. An angry argument broke out and they parted. After dinner Richard went out in the royal barge on the Thames. Between Lambeth and Westminster Richard met Courtenay in his boat and a conference took place on the water. Courtenay rather rashly repeated all that he had said previously. In a fury Richard drew his sword and was about to strike the archbishop when Richard's uncle, the Earl of Buckingham, restrained him. For some time after this Richard, out of sheer hatred of Courtenay, may well have refused to help the church.

Anne of Bohemia, Richard's wife and queen, was another important factor. She strongly favoured the Lollards and read the Scriptures in English. It is impossible to say what a restraining influence she quietly exercised on Richard. It was not until after her death (1394) that the penalty for heresy became death.

These restraining factors could not continue indefinitely. In the late summer of 1399, Richard lost his throne and Henry Bolingbroke, son of John of Gaunt, ascended it as Henry IV. Under him, England was to see harsher measures against the Lollards than it had so far done. In 1401 an infamous act for the burning of heretics was passed.

So far, as we have seen, no Lollard had been prepared to die for his faith. But a new generation of Lollards had now arisen. Some of them had such firm convictions that they were willing to face death itself. Swynderby came within a hair's breadth of death at Leicester, but the honour of being the Reformation's protomartyr was reserved for William Sawtrey,[2] a pious priest at St Margaret's, King's Lynn, Norfolk.

Sawtrey had the audacity to say, 'Instead of adoring the cross on which Christ suffered, I adore Christ who suffered on it.' He had preached against images and pilgrimages, and also rejected transubstantiation. Sawtrey was one of the few Lollards who appeared in Spencer's diocese. In 1399 he had been arrested by the bishop and been thrown into prison until he recanted. Upon his release, Sawtrey realized that he had been bullied into this denial of Christ. He went to London and soon began to preach Lollard doctrines. Here he found supporters who encouraged him and he grew more confident.

However, Courtenay's successor, Archbishop Arundel, was no less ruthless than Courtenay, and in February 1401, Sawtrey was summoned to the chapter house of St Paul's and confronted with his heresies. For over three hours Arundel questioned him on the doctrine of the mass and Sawtrey defended his position with scriptural arguments. He was determined not to deny the faith a second time. The doctrine of the mass was always the 'test question' for those accused of heresy. As Bishop Ryle says, 'On that doctrine, in almost every case, hinged their life or death.'[3] What happened in the early 1400s set the pattern for what would happen for another hundred and fifty years.

A relapsed heretic received no mercy, and a stubborn one like Sawtrey only appeared to be more guilty in the eyes of the hierarchy. His vestments and clerical clothes were torn off, his head shaved to remove the tonsure and a layman's cap placed on his head. Sawtrey was then handed over to the secular arm and, in accordance with the new statute, taken to Smithfield, where he was burned to death at the stake.

1. M. Brandt, 'Wyclifism in Dalmatia in 1383' in *Slavonic and East European Review* XXXVI (1957–58), pp. 58–68.
2. Also spelled 'Sautre', 'Sawtree' or 'Sawtre'.
3. J. C. Ryle, *Five English Reformers*, Banner of Truth Trust, 1960, p. 27.

16.
Later history of the Lollards (1401—1521)

1401–1521

In the space available it is impossible to give more than a small cameo of the history of the fifteenth-century Lollards. But the vital thing about their life and witness is seen in the way that they kept the clear light of truth burning. This was the lamp that Wycliffe had relit. At times it flickered and became faint; at others it shone forth brightly.

As we noted in the previous chapter, a new type and generation of Lollard had arisen. One of the last of the old generation, John Purvey, was tried for heresy in 1401. Purvey, although Wycliffe's friend and companion in his last years, could not face death by torture for his faith. After the years spent in the West Country (when he had completed his translation of the Bible), Purvey was at last caught and the hierarchy forced him either to abjure his faith and teaching or to burn. Purvey recanted. They then gave him a living where he was very unhappy. In 1403 he disappeared.

But it is worth noting that three days before Purvey read his recantation at St Paul's Cross, William Sawtrey had gone to the stake for stating that 'After consecration by the priest there remaineth true material bread.' Here was clear evidence of the new type of Lollard. They would suffer and die for the truth.

But how could people be burned for their faith in England? Persecution was a new thing here. This surely marked a change in the attitude of king and Parliament. The answer to this question and the turning-point of the Lollard cause is found in the accession of Henry IV. Henry Bolingbroke, son of John of Gaunt, had been banished from England. But when he landed in Yorkshire and recruited an army from the many malcontents who hated Richard, his victory was assured because the country rallied round him. Richard had made so many enemies that he could get no one to fight for him and was soon deposed and imprisoned in Pontefract Castle.

We saw the way that Courtenay sought to use the king to help the church but his successor, Arundel, was even more astute. A cunning priest and skilful politician, Arundel had deserted Richard and warmly welcomed Henry Bolingbroke. As he crowned Henry, he charged him to 'consolidate his throne, conciliate the clergy, and sacrifice the Lollards'. 'I will be the protector of the church,' promised Henry.

In the summer of 1399 Henry became king. Despite the proposals of the House of Commons to seize the lands and other wealth of the church to relieve taxation and aid the poor, Henry brushed these aside and in 1401 persuaded or cajoled both houses to pass a statute for the suppression of heresy. This infamous act, called *De Haeretico Comburendo,* authorized the burning of heretics, and William Sawtrey became England's protomartyr.

De Haeretico Comburendo remained on the statute book for many years. Henry V expanded it, Henry VIII repealed it, Mary revived it and Elizabeth I again repealed it. But while it remained a law, many people, men and women, young and old, suffered under it. Before this England had known little or nothing of the harsh punishments that the papal Inquisition administered in Europe. Largely through the royal claims and partly through the wish of the English prelates to retain some measure of independence, full papal jurisdiction had never been exercised in England. Heretics there had been, but not outstanding ones — until Wycliffe appeared. Those suspected of heresy were tried and examined by ecclesiastical courts. If guilty they had to abjure and do penance. Those who refused were excommunicated and normally imprisoned. If a heretic recanted and was caught as a relapsed heretic, he was then liable to the most severe punishment, death at the stake. Swynderby, who was saved by John of Gaunt, is an example of this, but such men were rare. Now under this new statute, they were to become only too common.

Later history of the Lollards

When Henry became king, there were two choices open to him: to follow Parliament's requests or obey the church. The influence of Wycliffe and the Lollards had gained a number of supporters in the Commons and, as mentioned above, demands had been made to seize church lands. While no spiritual reform would have taken place, some of the corruption could have been removed and lay emancipation could have commenced. But Henry chose to help the church and to build an even stronger dam against the rising waters of demands for reform. In the late fourteenth century and throughout the fifteenth century, the hierarchy refused even the smallest concession, ignored all need for reform and used brute force of the harshest kind. Their dam managed to hold back the rising waters throughout the fifteenth century, but soon after that it burst.

Many are horrified to read of the persecutions suffered in medieval times, but it should be noted that the doctrine of persecution was regarded as essential to medieval Christianity. It was a tradition that had persisted for roughly 1,000 years. Obedience to the doctrines of the church was regarded as essential, just as today obedience to the laws of the state is considered vital for the smooth running of the country. Religious persecution was like calling in the police in modern times. Toleration was an almost unknown word and those who persecuted the Lollards were not necessarily evil men. Persecution of dissenters was regarded as respectable and essential.

The trial and execution at the stake of heretics were called 'acts of faith' by the medieval church. We might well say that the 'act of faith' lay with the Lollard who had the courage to lay down his life rather than deny the truth. Soon after Henry's accession, the Archbishop of Canterbury drew up a list of articles called 'the Constitutions of Arundel'. These forbad the translation and reading of the Bible without the bishop's permission, and described the pope as 'not a mere man, but a true God'! This at a time when rival popes still excommunicated one another!

There appears to have been a slight hesitation on the part of the new king to make an all-out attack on the Lollards. Henry was probably somewhat afraid of the reaction of the knights of the shires who sat in the Commons. But in 1401 a Lollard tailor of Evesham named John Badby, in the diocese of Worcester, was arrested. Badby was dragged to London and tried before the full majesty of church and state. No less than two archbishops, eight bishops, the Duke of York and the Chancellor of England confronted him at his trial. Yet despite these imposing officials, Badby stood firm. He insisted that transubstantiation was impossible because 'Christ sitting at supper could not give his disciples his living body to eat'. Badby's trial shows clearly the value of men and women reading the Bible for themselves. His reasoning in his defence could not have taken place if he had not studied the Gospel account of the Last Supper.

Badby received no mercy. He was taken to Smithfield Market (the very place where young Richard had faced the peasants during the revolt) and tied to the stake. Young Prince Henry, though a strong supporter of the church, was not cruel and argued for a long time with Badby. He even promised him, not only his life, but money as well if he would recant.

It must have been an extraordinary scene: a humble tailor tied to the stake for his faith and the heir apparent to the throne of England begging him to recant. At one point Henry thought that he had succeeded. The faggots had been lit but the prince took Badby's contortions as he suffered as a sign that he would submit. The faggots were removed but to no avail. A second time the faggots were kindled and England's second martyr faced his death with courage. Henry later beat the French at Agincourt, but here, in his youth, he faced a man who was stronger than he: one whom he found to be beyond the power of bishops and kings.

The persecution spread and during the next 150 years, Smithfield saw many more martyrs. Some recanted, while others died in prison, but it appears that Sawtrey, and later Badby, were treated harshly to make them an example to other Lollards. But as persecution spread so, too, did Lollardy. Lincolnshire, Norfolk, Suffolk, Essex, Middlesex, Buckinghamshire and Somerset are counties to which the teaching spread during this century.

For some years after Wycliffe left Oxford, his teaching

Later history of the Lollards

still persisted at the university, but it had to be taught secretly. In 1395 some of the fellows of Merton College were arrested and the university ordered to root out any other heretics. But Oxford still honoured its late 'Evangelical Doctor'.

In 1406, however, communications between Peter Payne at Oxford and Prague University made it appear that Oxford still officially supported Wycliffe. This was too much for Arundel. He visited Oxford and held a convocation there in 1407. This convocation laid down strict rules for students, decided the subjects and contents of sermons to be preached and insisted that any discussion of the sacraments or articles of faith were to be strictly in accordance with the definitions laid down by Rome. It also formed a university committee to examine students monthly and expel any whose views were not one hundred per cent orthodox. It then forbad any new translations of the Bible and declared that existing ones must be used only after official permission had been granted. In 1411 Arundel forced the authorities at Oxford to take an oath to refuse entrance to all Lollards or suspected Lollards. Soon after this Payne fled to Bohemia to support Hus. The last nail in the coffin was the Council of Constance which, in 1415, condemned Wycliffe and all his writings 'lest they lead the faithful astray'. Oxford could no longer defend Wycliffe.

One of Swynderby's converts was no peasant but a knight of the shire and came from a good family. Sir John Oldcastle owned considerable property in West Herefordshire, the same district where Swynderby and others had successfully established a Lollard group. He earned the gratitude of Henry IV by maintaining order along the Welsh border. In 1409 Oldcastle married Joan, his third wife, who was heiress of Lord Cobham of Kent. This marriage later brought him, not only the title of Lord Cobham, but also estates and castles round the Thames and Medway, including Cowling Castle, where he lived. It is said that, because of his enthusiasm for the Wycliffite teaching, Oldcastle 'babbled' the Bible whenever opportunity offered. He certainly sheltered heretics and appointed Lollard priests to churches in Kent. Apart from this, he had correspondence with Hus in Bohemia.

Oldcastle was undoubtedly a man with deep religious convictions and much piety. Satirists expressed their feelings about his 'sanctimonious' ways in poems:

> It is unkindly for a knight,
>   That should a kinge's castle keep,
> To babble the Bible day and night
>   In resting time when he should sleep.

He took no pains to conceal his faith and became regarded by many as the leader of the Lollard cause. For years his friendship with Prince Henry apparently gave him immunity from any attack by the prelates. This seems to have gone to Oldcastle's head because he became openly scornful of the hierarchy and defiant in his ways.

Oldcastle lulled himself into a false sense of security. Henry IV died in March 1413 and no sooner had the accession of Henry V taken place than the situation changed. The young Henry was determined to crush Lollardy once and for all. Proceedings began against Oldcastle the same month as the old king died. Henry V wanted to show the country that no one, not even a man who enjoyed the king's friendship, could escape the flames if he became a Lollard.

The bishops attacked Oldcastle and subsequently Henry tried in vain to persuade him to recant. But the king found Oldcastle as steadfast and immovable as Badby. When summoned to appear before the ecclesiastical court, Oldcastle ignored the summons and declared that the church had no jurisdiction over him. He shut himself in Cowling Castle until the king sent a writ for his arrest. Oldcastle then surrendered.

He was brought under arrest to the bishops at St Paul's Chapter House (where Wycliffe had appeared in 1377). Sir John had not only understood Wycliffe's teaching, but had known the power of the Word in his life. He presented the bishops with a bold confession of his faith, in which he denounced the misuse of images and pilgrimages, rejected auricular confession and transubstantiation.

'As touching the pope and his spirituality', Oldcastle declared, 'I owe them neither suit nor service, forasmuch as I know him by the Scriptures to be the great Antichrist.'

His confession was thrust to one side, he was denounced as a heretic and handed over to the secular arm to be put to death. These were to be the standard proceedings under the new statute. Henry still hoped that Oldcastle would recant; to give him a further forty days' respite the king had him locked up in the Tower of London.

Meanwhile news of Oldcastle's arrest had spread throughout England. Lollards felt that the time had come for desperate measures. If they lost a supporter like this, they might be reduced to living in the woods or in caves. Very unwisely, they decided to take up arms against the king. Judged by the standards of those days, it was not necessarily wrong, since Henry was the son of a usurper, but with their small numbers and scant resources, they could never hope to win.

But during the night of 19 October 1413, three London Lollards 'spirited' Oldcastle out of the Tower. He went into hiding and sent messages to Lollard groups throughout the country. Oldcastle wanted them to converge on London and overthrow the government.

This attempted *coup* was doomed from its start. The plot was discovered and sixty Lollards, ranging from knight to artisan, were hanged as a penalty. A purge began in England to root out all Lollards. Oldcastle fled to the Welsh border with a price on his head. There he hid for three years. Finally, in late 1417, he was captured and sent to London for execution. His judges faced a problem: he was both a traitor and a heretic. Should he be hanged, beheaded or burned? Finally they decided that he must be hanged and burned simultaneously.

On the day of his execution, when Oldcastle appeared he looked remarkably cheerful. He was laid on a hurdle and dragged to St Giles' Field where a new gallows had been erected. Before his execution, Oldcastle fell down on his knees and asked God to forgive his enemies. He then addressed the crowd, exhorted them to follow the laws of God and to beware of false teachers. He was then hung up by the middle with chains of iron and burned to death, praising God to the last.

This attempted rebellion drove the Lollards underground yet it did not destroy them. But the main reason for their survival was that they had become a popular movement.

They were anti-clerical, encouraged lay piety and were mainly concerned with that vital inner spirituality which the medieval church in general lacked.

The case of Sir John Oldcastle is the one notable exception to the rigid class division in the persecution of the Lollards. This division persisted down to the Reformation. In those days it was unthinkable that people of noble blood should be tried for their religious convictions. But for the peasants, artisans and yeomen, it was a different matter.

Despite persecution, however, the Lollards continued to spread, although mainly among the working people. In 1431 the Bishop of Bath and Wells declared that he would excommunicate any who either translated the Bible or copied such a translation.

About the time of Henry VI's accession (1422) East Anglia, where Bishop Spencer had persecuted the Lollards or scared them away, was overrun with them. Large congregations were formed on the borders of Norfolk and Suffolk. Lollard schools were started and heretical tracts smuggled in from London.

This did not go unnoticed, and they endured much persecution and suffering. But they were like the Christians mentioned in Acts 8:4: 'Those who had been scattered preached the word wherever they went.' They made many converts. Some merely gave mental assent to their teaching, but there must have been a number who, like Badby and Oldcastle, had a real living faith in Christ. The Lollards faced a problem that Luther and the other Reformers were to meet: it is easy to gain supporters when preaching against the apostasy and corruption of the church, but it is difficult to bring people to see the truth of the doctrine of justification by faith.

For proof of the success of the Lollards, the somewhat unusual attack made on them by Reginald Pecock, Bishop of Chichester, must be noted. Unlike most ecclesiastics of that time (1450), Pecock wrote a book to confute their teachings. He attempted to reason, not in Latin, but in English, and appealed to the reason of laymen and showed that, to him, Wycliffe's teaching was not only heretical but foolish. To justify such a book as this (before printing had commenced in England) there must surely have been many Lollards living in England and they cannot all have been illiterate.

Pecock attacked the use of Bible texts which the 'lay party' used and pointed out that their interpretation of these texts was strained and wrong. In his book called *The Repressor of Overmuch Blaming the Clergy*, he proves to his own satisfaction that Scripture does not forbid the practices of the church.

For his effort to 'defend the faith', Pecock was tried for heresy in 1457. He was accused of rejecting the authority of the old doctors of the church, and of having said that no writings were to be accepted unless they were agreeable to reason. Pecock appears to have been a rationalist to a large extent. For this he was condemned and had either to recant or burn. He had no living faith like Oldcastle and recanted. His public abjuration was read at St Paul's Cross, he lost his bishopric and was confined to Thorney Abbey to end his days. If an intelligent and orthodox man like Pecock could be tried for heresy, what hope was there for any Lollard who was caught?

Yet despite the penalties, the movement continued to spread. The ever-increasing number of people put to death for their Lollard teachings shows that the flame lit by Wycliffe still burnt steadily. The registers of persecuting bishops show that a good number of Lollard congregations still existed between 1490 and 1521. Apart from the Lollard Bible, Wycliffe's *Wicket,* the tract against transubstantiation, was most widely used and discussed.

Even Erasmus, when writing to Pope Adrian VI in 1523, confessed that 'Once the party of the Wycliffites was overcome by the power of the kings; but it was only overcome and not extinguished.'

'Not extinguished.' The Lollards had played their part. They had faithfully kept the light of the gospel burning for nearly one and a half centuries. Their work was almost complete. The Reformation had begun.

Monument to Wycliffe at Lutterworth.

Bibliography

Bettenson, H. (ed.), *Documents of the Christian Church*, Oxford University Press, 1946.
Boettner, L., *Roman Catholicism*, Presbyterian and Reformed Publishing Co., 1962.
Bruce, F. F., *The English Bible*, Lutterworth Press, 1961.
Bruce, F. F., *The Spreading Flame*, Paternoster Press, 1958.
D'Aubigné, J. H. Merle, *The Reformation in England* (Vol. I), (ed. S. M. Houghton), Banner of Truth Trust, 1962.
Fraser, Antonia (ed.), *The Lives of the Kings and Queens of England*, Weidenfeld and Nicolson, 1975.
Le Bas, C. W., *Life of Wiclif*, 1832.
Parker, G. H. W., *The Morning Star*, Paternoster Press, 1965.
Ryle, J. C., *Five English Reformers*, Banner of Truth Trust, 1960.
Trevelyan, G. M., *England in the Age of Wycliffe*, Longmans, Green and Co. Ltd, 1925.
Trevelyan, G. M., *English Social History*, Longmans, Green and Co. Ltd, 1944.
Trevelyan, G. M., *History of England*, Longmans, Green and Co. Ltd, 1926.
Vaughan, Robert, *John de Wycliffe, D.D.*, 1853.
Walker, W., *A History of the Christian Church*, Morrison and Gibb Ltd, 1918.
Wilson, Derek, *The People and the Book*, Barries and Jenkins Ltd, 1976.

Index

Aldhelm, Bishop, 78
Anne of Bohemia, Queen, 91, 109, 124
Arundel, Archbishop, 119, 125, 128, 129, 131
Aston, John, 87, 100, 101, 103, 104, 121, 122, 123
Augustine, Archbishop of Canterbury, 5
Augustine, Bishop of Hippo, 13, 81
Avignon, Papacy ('Babylonian Captivity'), 22, 45, 46–47, 59, 75–76, 107
Badby, John, 130, 132, 134
Becket, Thomas à (Archbishop of Canterbury), 33, 44, 94
Bede, Venerable, 79
Bible (Scriptures) –
    authority and sufficiency of, 77, 116, 117
    Rome's attitude to, 79, 80, 129
    translation of, 69, 77, 78–79, 89–91, 117, 120, 134
    widespread ignorance of, 40
    Wycliffe's, 78, 90–91, 99, 127
    Wycliffe's view of, 40–41, 52, 68–69, 77–78, 86, 116–117
Bishops –
    appointment of, 23, 33, 44–45
    persecution of Lollards by, 132, 134
    Wycliffe's appearances before, 51–53, 66–68
Black Death, 8, 10, 13, 81, 92
Black Prince (Edward), 36, 39, 49, 54, 55, 67
Blackfriars, Synod of, 90, 96–97, 99, 100, 101, 104
Bohemians, 109–110, 131
Bradwardine, Thomas, 12–13, 14, 81
Calvin, John, 42, 82, 116
Canterbury Hall, wardenship of, 21, 23–24, 32
Cardinals, 68, 70, 75–76, 116
Charlemagne, Emperor, 22, 54
Church –
    British (English), 1, 4–6, 18, 30, 62
    doctrine of (ecclesiology), 114–116
    Greek, 4, 7, 75, 115
    Roman, 3–4, 9, 12, 22, 34–35, 75, 79, 80, 81, 88, 110
    Roman, Wycliffe's attitude to, 31–32, 34, 49, 64–65, 67, 77, 88, 114–115
Clergy, 3, 5, 6, 9, 11, 16–18, 20, 38–39, 73, 88

Clergy, appointment of, 43—45
Commons, House of — see Parliament
Confession, sacrament of, 44, 81, 114, 115
Constance, Council of, 111, 119
Constantine, Emperor, 2—3
Consubstantiation, doctrine of, 84, 116
Courtenay, Bishop, later Archbishop, 49—50, 51—56, 59—61, 63, 64, 66—67,
    71, 95, 96—98, 100, 101, 103—105, 118, 121, 123—124, 125, 128
De Haeretico Comburendo, Statute, 128
Decalogue (Ten Commandments), 40—41
Edward III, King, 10, 26—27, 36, 38, 45, 49, 56, 60—61
Election, doctrine of, 13—14, 81—82, 113
Erastianism, doctrine of, 73
Eucharist (Holy Communion, Lord's Supper, the mass), doctrine of, 7, 77,
    82—84, 88, 91, 98, 101, 107, 116, 121, 123, 125
Excommunication, 29, 34, 45, 65, 67, 84, 115, 124, 128, 134
Foxe, John, 37, 42
France —
    relationship with papacy, 22, 28, 29, 107, 109
    war against, 26—27, 36, 48, 54, 57—58, 93, 107—108
Friars, 9, 11, 14, 15—19, 44, 86, 88, 98, 100, 101, 107
Friars, Wycliffe's relationship with, 18—19, 25, 34, 73—74, 84
Grosseteste, Robert, 11, 12, 17
Haule, 70—72
Henry II, King, 32—33, 44
Henry IV, King (Bolingbroke), 104, 125, 127—129, 131—132
Henry V, King, 128, 130, 132—133
Henry VIII, King, 60, 65, 97, 99, 128
Hereford, Nicholas, 87, 99—102, 103, 123
Hus, John, 110, 111, 119, 131
Indulgences, papal, 86, 114
Inquisition, papal, 69, 104, 128
Interdict, papal, 29
John of Gaunt — see Lancaster, Duke of
John, King, 26—27, 28—30, 32, 43, 46, 66
Justification by faith, doctrine of, 64—65, 81, 113, 114
Lancaster, Duke of (John of Gaunt), 10, 36—37, 39, 44, 46, 48—49, 50, 51—56,
    57—59, 65, 66, 71—72, 84, 85, 93—94, 96, 99, 103, 121, 125, 128
Langham, Archbishop 21
Lateran Council, Fourth, 83
Lollards (poor priests), 53, 86—88, 90, 91, 95, 97, 100, 103, 104, 106, 111,
    112, 118—126, 127—135
London —
    confrontation of citizens with John of Gaunt, 54—56, 57—58
    earthquake, 97
    Lollards in, 101, 118, 125, 130
    Peasants' Revolt, 93—94
    Wycliffe in, 50, 51, 53, 66—67
Luther, Martin, 13, 41, 42, 47, 62, 75, 82, 84, 108, 110, 112, 113, 114, 116, 134

Index

Lutterworth, 47–48, 87, 102, 103, 104, 105, 106, 110, 123
Magna Carta (Great Charter), 27, 30, 92, 104
Mass — see Eucharist
Melanchthon, Philip, 113
Monks, 9, 10, 16–18, 21, 25, 34–36, 98
Normans, 7, 17, 33, 43, 79, 83
Oldcastle, Sir John (Lord Cobham), 120, 131–133, 134, 135
Oxford, Convocation of, 104, 131
Oxford, city of, 39–40
Oxford, University of —
    attitude to Wycliffe's teaching, 19, 35, 42, 59, 62–64, 65, 87, 89–90, 97–100, 101, 104–105, 106, 120, 131
    Wycliffe at, 10, 11, 13, 19, 20–21, 26, 56, 68, 73, 84–85, 91
Papacy, doctrine of, 3–4, 6–7, 9, 12, 22, 27–28, 31–32, 47, 60–62, 64–65, 68, 76, 115, 116, 129, 132
Parliament —
    and the church, 9, 18–19, 26–27, 35, 36, 44–46, 48, 54, 60, 69, 71, 96, 108, 128
    the 'Good...', 48–49, 53
    and the Lollards, 118, 120, 127, 128
    Magna Carta, 30
    Wycliffe and, 25, 31, 32, 37, 61–63, 66, 85, 103–104, 106
Peasants' Revolt, 91–95, 96, 98, 99, 107
Pecock, Bishop, 134, 135
Pelagianism, doctrine of, 13, 81, 113
Percy, Lord, 50, 51–53, 54, 55, 58, 66
Perrers, Alice, 49
Pope (see also Papacy, doctrine of)
    Wycliffe's appeal to, 21, 23
    Wycliffe's meeting with, 46, 47
Praemunire, Statutes of, 27, 45
Predestination, doctrine of, 13, 82, 95, 113
Presbyterianism, doctrine of, 60, 65, 116
Priests, 4, 6–7, 9, 11, 21, 29, 38, 82–83, 98, 102, 107
Provisors, Statute of, 18, 27, 45
Purgatory, doctrine of, 89, 114
Puritans, 42, 88
Purvey, John, 90, 110, 120, 122, 123, 127
Reformation, 4, 12, 73, 80, 81, 82, 125, 134, 135
Repingdon, Philip, 100, 101, 103, 104
Repton, Philip, 87
Richard II, King, 56, 57–58, 61, 65, 71, 91, 92, 94–95, 103, 109, 123, 124–125, 128, 130
Rome (see also Church, Roman), 47, 48, 59, 60, 61, 66, 67, 70, 75–76, 81, 88, 96, 98, 102, 111
Rome, Bishop of, see Papacy, Pope
Rygge, Robert, 99, 100–101, 104
Sanctuary, right of, 70–72
Sawtrey, William, 125–126, 127, 128, 130

Schism, Great, 70, 75—77
Scholasticism, 14, 34, 77
Shakell, 70—71
Smithfield, 126, 130
Spencer, Bishop, 107—108, 125, 134
Students, 14—15, 39, 40
Sudbury, Archbishop, 50, 53, 59, 63—64, 66, 71—72, 93, 94, 95, 96
Swynderby, William, 120—121, 125, 128, 131
Tower of London, 71, 93, 94, 133
Transubstantiation, doctrine of, 83—84, 97, 101, 116, 125, 130, 135
Valencia, Council of, 80, 117
Vatican, 63, 64
Vulgate (Latin Bible), 78, 89
Waldensians, 69, 88
Walsingham (monastic chronicler), 53, 57, 67, 68, 112
Westminster Abbey, 70—71
William the Conqueror, 7, 11, 43, 79
Wycliffe, John —
    appearance, 53
    banished from Oxford, 100, 104—105
    birth and early life, 7, 9—10
    bishops, appearances before, 50, 51—53, 66—68, 70
    condemnation by church, 59—60, 64, 84—85, 111, 119, 120, 131
    death, 111, 112, 120
    friars and monks, relations with, 18, 19, 25—26, 28, 32, 34—35, 98
    Fillingham, rector of, 20, 24
    importance of his work, 1, 42, 112, 127, 135
    influence in Bohemia, 110
    and the Lollards, 86—89, 102—103, 129
    Ludgershall, rector of, 24, 47
    at Lutterworth, 47, 48, 87, 91, 102, 104—105, 106, 111
    meeting with pope, 46—47
    at Oxford, 10, 11—15, 19, 20—21, 24, 26, 39, 48, 56, 63—64, 68, 69, 84—85, 100
    and Parliament, 37, 54, 61—62, 64, 85, 108
    public opinion of, 53, 55, 56, 64, 69
    receives deputation of friars, 73—74
    'sanctuary', views on, 70, 72
    teachings (see also 'writings'), 65, 72—73, 81—84, 89, 95, 101, 102, 112—117, 122, 132, 134
    translation of the Bible, 78, 80, 89—91
    warden of Canterbury Hall, 21, 23—24, 32
    writings, 31—33, 34, 38—39, 40—42, 49, 62, 68, 72, 76—77, 80, 82, 84, 108—109, 110, 135
Wykeham, Bishop, 36, 37, 39, 49, 53, 56, 57, 100